THE LOST PRODIGAL

Joel Rodriguez

JR Legacy
PUBLISHING

ISBN-13:

979-8-9905232-0-3 -Paperback
979-8-9905232-1-0- Hardcover
979-8-9905232-2-7 eBook

Library of Congress Control Number: 2024911261

J R Legacy Publishing
Freehold, New Jersey

Typeset by: Michelle Cline

CONTENTS

ACKNOWLEDGMENTS

To Carmen, my beloved wife, whose unfailing love,
support, and encouragement helped shape my heart and
mind in order to produce this book. To my better half,
I thank you again for your love and ever-present devotion
over the last thirty-seven years.

To my daughter, Cheyenne, who has been an
amazing source of inspiration, pride, and joy.
You are truly uniquely and wonderfully made.

To my family, whose immense love, support,
and prayers have led me along the way. You've all lived
exemplary lives, and I praise God for each of you daily.

To all children, especially the prodigal sons and daughters.
Don't wait until it's too late to return home.
Tomorrow is not promised to anyone.

FOREWORD

The gospel message displays God's love and heart for the lost. In Luke 15:11–32, we see the parable of a young man whose decision to take his inheritance before his time led him to self-suffering that brought him to a place of despair and unmanageability. Suffering the consequences of his choices, he soon experienced the agony associated, which reckless living guarantees. The Lost Prodigal left a place of abundance and found himself in great poverty and need. Being separated from his family by his own doing, he realized that the misery he was experiencing was by his own hand. The downward spiral led him to come to an awakening that changed the direction of his life. Once the Lost Prodigal came to his senses, he realized that there was more than abundance in his father's house. Acceptance of his wrongdoing led the Lost Prodigal to accept the importance of accountability and surrender. The decision to return home came from a place of conviction and repentance. As the young prodigal son approached far along in his journey home, he found himself face-to-face with his father, who was waiting for his safe return. Unconditional acceptance and love revealed the father's heart. How amazing it is to witness such profound love and grace. In this book, *The Lost Prodigal*, we embark on the story of Joel Rodriguez's life. This amazing testimony parallels the parable of the prodigal son in many ways, living a life of crime, abuse, and reckless living, which caused heartache and devastation in Joel's life. Joel's relationships were affected by the type of lifestyle he was living. However, hitting rock bottom gave Joel the birth of a new spiritual beginning. The author's heart to share his story with the world stems from a place of love for the lost. We read the conviction that restoration and forgiveness are possible for those who surrender to Christ. *The Lost Prodigal* is a story that bears witness to a man's journey in search of growth and witness of God's goodness. Joel stood on God's promises, which broke the chains and cycles of addictions. In this story, the author speaks about a letter he wrote to God in solitary confinement in that dark and lonely cell. Out of desperation, the author pens his heart on that paper, crying out to God for rescue and intervention. As a prison chaplain, I, too, have witnessed the pain and sorrow of men and women lost in the system and the cycle of addictive lifestyles. God answered Joel's prayers and granted him a new life. If you don't believe in miracles, I encourage you to read this book and witness the redemptive power that God offers the lost through His Son, Jesus Christ.

Pastor Cleo Santiago, BCCC, BCPC, GRMS, Chaplain, Hospice Care & Hudson County Department of Corrections & Rehabilitation Center

A LETTER TO GOD

Dear God:
Another pain filled day has come and went where are all those blessings you supposively sent. I'm going crazy, I'm losing my mind, didn't you once say seek and you shall find. Yet I look all around me, I look up above, I've no where left to look and still can't find your love. Oh Lord my God where have you gone, no matter where I look your no where to be found. What have I done that was so bad, what was the cause of making you mad. Lord God in heaven Lord God above, what ever happened to all that love? you promised to never leave me nor forsake me, but I know you've turned your face beacuse I can't feel your presence in this filthy, lonely place. Day by day I endure such pain, oh Lord my God keep me from going insane. I thought I did right by going to trial, cause eventhough I lost I'd see your glory in just a little while. But as I've waited thus so long, the affliction I encounter forces

me to sing this sad, lonely song. Yes, I did a crime I shouldn't of tried and that I've never denied. Yet the crime I committed was against the state and they decided my worldly fate-to prison I was sent; but against you God I have sinned and of that I do repent. As I sit and write you from my lonely prison cell, I think to myself, at least I'm not in hell. At least I'll have a chance to make things right and I know you'll bless me in my plight. So, though I nag and complain, deep down I know its you whose kept me sane. As I end this letter, I regain my common-sence and once again feel your holy presence. Maybe I was in error to write you this letter, but strangely enough I feel a little better. Next time I'll try as your word says to do. I promise to obey, get on my knees and pray, each and every single day. Well Lord for now I'll say good-night for I know tomorrow holds another spiritual fight: but as long as I know that your near, ain't a demon on earth that I'm gonna fear.

Your son Joel

(One dark, lonely night during year six: Dec. 1995)
Written during fifteen days in solitary confinement

I

ROOTS: WE ALL HAVE A BEGINNING

My story begins just before the Great Depression of 1929 with my parents. My father was born in June 1922 on the poorly developed island of Puerto Rico. The reality is that even though I am a published author today, I come from a father who was forced to drop out of school as a young boy. When he was in third grade, his mother died; thus, my father dropped out in order to take care of the home while his brother and father worked to provide for the family. As a result, my father never learned how to read or write and essentially grew up semi-literate. Unfortunately, I never had the opportunity to meet his father. Family is every-thing, and at its core are foundational beliefs, values, and customs, which form building blocks for cohesive future generations. My beautiful mother was born in June 1929 into a family of fourteen children. Her family resided in a sugar cane shack provided to them by the owner of the farm in return for my grandparents' labor. Despite abject poverty, my mother and her siblings attempted to better their economic condition by educating themselves as best they could. My mother attended a college in Puerto Rico until she was discharged for lack of tuition funding, but the benefit of having achieved a level of education of at least high school would allow her to communicate well and help pave the way and establish some form of decent life in the United States.

My mother and father both arrived at the United States in the 1940s. When my mother arrived, she went to live with her aunt Sofia, whose husband was a pastor of a small Pentecostal church (*Iglesia Cristiana Misionera*/Christian Missionary Church, 247 7th Street, New York, NY) on the Lower East Side of Manhattan. My mother served as *au pair* to her five cousins while attending church faithfully; subsequently, she met my father, and soon after, they fell in love. Money was always tight for my parents. They had no vices and devoted all of their time, talents, and treasure to the Lord and their ever-growing family.

My siblings and I grew up in the New York City Housing Authority's Baruch Housing Complex in a three-bedroom apartment on the eighth floor. It is difficult to believe that nine people were cramped into three bedrooms, with one bathroom, no cable TV, cell phones, internet, or air-conditioning. My father made very little money, so little that we qualified and received full welfare benefits, including food stamps. Additionally, my mother would visit the government subsidy center, where they periodically provided us with a five-pound can of peanut butter, powdered eggs, and a block of cheese. My father had four occupations: husband, breadwinner, and church bus driver, combined with ushering at our local congregation. My father was blessed to be employed just a few blocks from our home in a largely Jewish cooperative complex, where he recovered used mattresses, furniture, and even clothing. We struggled financially, but everyone around us were predominately in the same economic position, so we never really noticed how poor we really were. We were never exposed to the finer things in life. We didn't realize we were being deprived of things and were content to have food on the table and clothes on our backs, even if they were slightly used. We went to church meetings several times a week and learned morals and values that we treasure to this day. My dad drove the church bus, and as a result, he was in church activities every day. This meant: Monday for prayer service, Tuesday for men's service, Wednesday for home service, Thursday—even though it was a women's service, he had to drive the bus, Friday for youth service, Saturday for children's service, and Sunday was, well, Sunday school in the morning and the evangelistic service Sunday evening. My dad woke up each morning at 6 a.m. and was out by 7 a.m. He returned each day at 4:30 p.m., ate, took a nap, and would leave for the church meetings around 6:30 p.m. He usually made it home by 10:30 p.m. and did it all again the next day, without skipping a beat. My father modeled 1 Timothy 5:8: "But if anyone does not provide for his relatives, and especially for members of his household, he has denied the faith and is worse than an unbeliever."

FINDING MY WAY

My beautiful mother cared for us seven kids as best she could, feeding us, teaching us, and blessing us with the occasional discipline we deserved. Of all the children, I got it the most and was the brat of the bunch. I look back now and attribute it to attention-seeking behavior. I was the fourth of seven children. This would be considered the middle child. The boys and girls were evenly matched except for me. The order of birth was Daniel, David, Rebecca, Joel, Esther, Joshua, and Elias. Everyone was essentially paired off except for me. I was too old to hang with Joshua, Elias, or Esther and too young to hang with Daniel, David, or Rebecca. That left me with skipping rope or finding friends to hang with outside of the family unit. I was born on October 9th, 1960, during the peak of the civil rights struggle. You have to understand all of the things that were happening around us during these crucial years. For example, this was the same year that four Black students sat down at a Whites-only lunch counter in Greensboro, North Carolina, in February 1960 and refused to leave. In fact, I was three years old when President John F. Kennedy was murdered. In 1960, I was born into a world that had just decided Brown v. Board of Ed. just six years earlier. I was five-years-old when Malcolm X was assassinated and eight years old when Dr. Martin Luther King and Bobby Kennedy were killed. Everything around me seemed like war and chaos. I recall how I would venture out on my own when I was very young and didn't understand why I felt out of place. I got bullied and pushed around a few times and really had no one in my corner. Fortunately, I had something my siblings didn't, and that was my size. Being left alone a lot meant that my dad would often take me to work with him. Sweeping floors, mopping, and distributing promotional flyers were welcomed distractions and an opportunity to earn a few bucks. I soon began to lift weights, tone my body, and learn the streets. I was very careful not to get involved in the bad stuff because my parents always taught us that even if they were not around, God was always watching, and this fear of the Lord kept us in line for much of our childhood.

I was always getting my behind whipped (physically disciplined) at home. During the earlier part of my *whipping days,* I would run to the bathroom and lock the door. Needless to say, it was the only bathroom in the house, so this created quite an inconvenience as I refused to come out until Mom cooled off. It was quite a negotiating tool! It was so funny watching my mother and brothers try to gain access to the bathroom. No one knew how I had the strength to hold them off. The truth is my mother kept a mop in the bathroom, and I just propped it from the bottom of the commode to the crease of an inner panel on the door. "Child rights," you say? The belt was the judge and jury at home. One day, my mother was called into my school due to a complaint by my sixth-grade teacher, and I was wearing a yellow shirt that day. I recall saying, *"Oh no, you're a liar"* to the teacher, and next thing I knew, *"fuácata"*—that was the noise of my mother smacking me across the face, impacting my nose so severely that I began to bleed and continued so for some time. By this time, I had been rushed into the office; the teachers and students who ventured in would look at me with a state of shock. There I was in a blood-soaked yellow shirt, tilting my head back until the bleeding stopped. "Child services," you say? Your parents were child services during those days! I continued to act out and barely made it through junior high school. In fact, I never graduated; I was officially transferred to high school. My behavior was really bad, but my artistic ability was impressive, and I made it into the High School of Art & Design. It was a hard school to get into, and I took it for granted. No one really counseled me about losing such a valuable opportunity and the boost it could give to my desire to become an architect. All I could see was that it was a school full of nerds and, in addition, I wasn't sure if I could do six years of college afterward. I slacked off and was kicked out of this specialized high school and sent to my zone school, Seward Park High. I only lasted a few months and dropped out. I figured that since my dad had raised seven kids and maintained a home without a high school degree, I could do it too.

During these years, my parents had anxiously awaited a transfer to a larger ground-floor apartment, and one day it came through. We moved downstairs to a four-bedroom apartment with a much larger living room and kitchen. Meanwhile, my older brothers both worked in the garment industry and sold small quantities of illegal drugs out of the ground-floor window. They would also steal fabric from their employer and have suits, shirts, and pants tailor-made. They were nicknamed the Super Fly Brothers by some in the hood. I simply enjoyed the unique hand-me-downs which gave me notoriety in junior high school. As I got older, my brothers asked me to basically mind the store, essentially selling joints and nickel bags out of the window while they were out. My brother Dan would pay me a buck a bag and would tell me that he paid Dave in drugs but did not want me using substances and would only pay me in cash. This went on until I was in my teens and lasted until my brothers converted to Christianity and gave their hearts to Jesus. The irony is that their conversion gave way to my opportunity to pick up where they had left off and take over their client base. The only thing that changed was the location of the window and the amount of pot you could now purchase. I never really had role models my age, and no one gave me career guidance or advice. In fact, all those years of watching my brothers sling drugs while living at home made things easy, so I dropped out of school and worked as a janitor while selling drugs, despite my father's philosophy of "Go to school and grab the opportunity I didn't have, so if you still want to be a bum, be an educated bum." I thought I knew best; little did I know of the reckoning that was coming just around the corner. I was becoming a lost and oblivious prodigal. The dictionary defines *oblivious* as not aware of or not concerned about what is happening around you. It defines lost as no longer possessed or retained; no longer to be found; having gone astray or missed the way; bewildered as to place, direction and lastly, being something that someone has failed to win.

The two combined imply a thickheaded imperviousness to ideas and openness to catastrophe. When I was about sixteen, my dad found his long-lost son "John." In an effort to repair their relationship and introduce him into our family, Dad had him flown down from Puerto Rico to stay with us. I remember John was in is his thirties and was shy and withdrawn for the first few days. My dad managed to help find him work, and that's when the monster began to arise from within. He began coming home drunk more and more frequently, and his true character was now exposed. My father attempted to counsel him, but it had no effect. I recall one payday had rolled around, and he disappeared. After several days, he showed up stripped clean of any money or valuables, and his shoes were also missing. Shortly thereafter, my dad gave him an ultimatum, and he apparently chose to return to Puerto Rico, abandon his family, and dishonor his father. It was a difficult lesson, which I only would later understand that alcohol addiction played a large part in his irrational and chaotic decision-making.

Bottom line, Satan tries everything at his disposal, drugs, sexual immorality, manipulation, or plain old envy and desire, and one thing's for sure, the prodigal effect is real.

One of my father's most profound and unforgettable phrases was, "Joel, yu ise no eres sdu-pid, huh?" Meaning, "Joel, you aren't really stupid, are you?" Furthermore, the word *stupid* and *stupidity* appear in the Bible some two dozen times. Proverbs 12:1 says, "The person who loves correction loves knowledge, but anyone who hates a rebuke is stupid." Jeremiah 10:14–16 says, "Everyone is stupid and without knowledge." Proverbs 15:21 says, "Stupidity is the delight of the senseless, but an understanding man walks uprightly." Jeremiah 4:22 says, "For my people are foolish; they know me not; they are stupid children." Proverbs 17:11–12 says, "A rebellious person seeks evil; a cruel emissary will be sent to oppose him. It's better to meet a mother bear who has lost her cubs than a fool in his stupidity." Just to name a few verses that speak to and recognize lapses of judgment and moments of recklessness, impulsivity, and foolishness. This certainly described a long and dark stage of my life. I was sadly a stupid prodigal. I was not conscientiously paying proper attention to many important things. I was also completely ignoring the dangers, risks, and consequences of life. I never imagined that in the years to come, I would be covered in a dark cloud of oblivion and chaos of my own making, where, just like my lost brother John, I would misconstrue and be confused by many things. Above all, I never thought that many years later I would produce a child who would also be likewise challenged by a dark cloud of oblivion and turmoil that would bring about a great deal of confusion and despair and ultimately consequences. Proverbs 20:24 says, "A man's steps are *ordained* by the LORD; How then can a person understand his way."

2
LOVE AND MARRIAGE

After my brothers' conversion, they decided to sit, abide, and fellowship under the leadership of Rev. Angel Rivera when he transferred his pastoral call from a little church on the *Lower East Side* to *La Iglesia Bethel*, a small Pentecostal church on 110th Street in New York City. I also followed along, but not for the same reasons. I had met a girl, Esperanza "Cookie" Martinez, during a service there and soon began visiting her at her home on Adam Clayton Powell Boulevard in Spanish Harlem/New York City. I had lived a somewhat sheltered life, and the excitement of traveling uptown to see my girlfriend intrigued me. She was an adventurous young girl with little restraint. She was from the hood like me but was quite a defiant individual, and I never had a girlfriend who was like this. She was a bit rough around the edges and independent, and her parents didn't have that old-fashioned discipline I had grown to understand as my norm. Being a know-it-all at eighteen years of age, I didn't listen to the advice of those who told me the girl was trouble and that I should stay away. Additionally, Harlem was my drug market, where I would purchase pounds of pot at discounted rates and resell it. While engaged in this new level of risk-taking, Esperanza and I became pregnant. I did the honorable thing and got an apartment for us on the Lower East Side of Manhattan, Ludlow Street, right off of Delancey. I tried providing for us as best I could but found myself getting nowhere at times.

I started to work in construction and demolition and became a shoe salesman, luggage salesman, and even a janitor, all that the "uneducated and unskilled" were qualified for as per the societal norms those days. Eventually, I landed a job as a security guard. Soon, I was making decent cash and providing for my daughter Jennifer (Jai) and her mother. I remember buying Jennifer all the latest educational toys, *Speak & Spell, Speak & Read,* and *Speak & Math*, and Esperanza, who spoke Ebonics, would say, "I don't knows why you buys her all that? You trying to make her into a Rodriguez!" Yes, I absolutely was! I wanted her to have a better life and manage it much more positively than her parents had. I come from the hood as well and could speak Ebonics also, but I wanted my daughter Jai to excel in every dimension of her life.

We had our issues like many new, struggling families, headed by eighteen-year-old parents. We were too young, immature, and naïve, to say the least. I worked hard to maintain for our little family. I did what was expected of me and thought things were going well, and then one day, I noticed Esperanza was being sneaky and evasive. I searched her belongings and discovered that she was having an affair. I felt betrayed, confused, and bewildered. I confronted her regarding her trustworthiness and her actions of putting us at risk by being intimate with some other man. I couldn't get over it, and it came to the point to which I subsequently left her. She begged and pleaded to no avail since I was afraid she may have brought home a disease and placed us all in jeopardy. Meanwhile, I continued to work for a private security firm where my sister Rebecca was employed as a secretary. I did security everywhere, at the Palladium, Roseland, and Bonds International, in addition to building/perimeter security; the worst assignments were supermarkets because I hated to bust little old ladies stealing cat food. I plunged myself into work, and it was a welcomed distraction while I tried to move past the deceit and deception. I was emotionally devastated, and in the middle of my pain and suffering, I met a sweet young banker who made a life-changing impact on my life. My new girl lived far, near the end of the "A" line, and I would buy a six-pack for the subway ride, which made it more tolerable. As I traveled home one night, a White, apparently racist K9 cop pulled me off the train. I had finished my beers and had no drugs on me. I had forgotten my girl's mother had given me some herbs and ginger root wrapped in aluminum foil, which was in my back pocket. The cop handcuffed me and took me to a vacant bathroom. Now, while handcuffed, he set the K9 dog to attack mode, and the dog went nuts, tearing and ripping into my jeans, all while his fellow cops looked on and laughed while the attack took place. There are honorable police officers, and there are dishonorable and disgraceful cops, and these were the latter. Upon discovering that I had nothing on me, they threatened me and told me to get lost. My hands and legs were bleeding from all the dog bites and scratches, and my clothes were in shreds, so I immediately went to my neighborhood precinct on the way home. The cop at the front desk was dismissive and gave me lip about it being out of their jurisdiction and so on; needless to say, this abusive and criminal encounter left an indelible, traumatic impression that haunts me until today. God has tried to mold me to trust police more; fortunately, the law enforcement brothers in the faith I've gotten to know have given me hope that change is possible.

Sometime later, Esperanza was so desperate to reconcile that she went to live with my family in Puerto Rico, hoping I would change my mind. Sadly, I felt so betrayed and violated that I could not bring myself to trust her again and informed her that I had met someone else and suggested that she do the same. Today, I feel that I should have had a more forgiving heart, even though Psalm 55:11 states, "Destruction is in her midst; Oppression and deceit do not depart from her streets." We are called to love and forgive each other, and I was wrong to not have allowed it to begin with me.

NOT HOW I THOUGHT IT WOULD BE

Esperanza and my daughter Jai lived at my parents' home in Rio Grande, Puerto Rico, for some time. One day, she informed me she had met a guy named Rey R, and she wanted to tell me that she planned to marry him. I congratulated her and even sent her a thousand dollars as a wedding present and gave her my blessing. She gave me some sad, tearful story, saying: "Thank you, Joe. Thank you and your family for the support all this time. Thank you for helping me move on peacefully. I promise I will never keep you from your daughter." But as we all know, we are all capable of breaking promises. She arrived back in New York as Mrs. Rivera and, unfortunately, started to withhold my daughter Jai. She began to alienate my family and me from my daughter and began to use the separation as a tool to inflict pain on me and confuse Jai, who was just five, more and more.

Sometimes I was able to have my weekend visit, and other times, I lost the opportunity because Esperanza simply wouldn't allow it, and what was worse, I started to get the impression that my daughter was being emotionally abused and confused. I remember how she would tell my daughter that if she came with me, she wouldn't be there when she got back. Other times, she would reject her and tell her that if she loved me, she could not love her mother also. Imagine pushing your daughter away and essentially rejecting her if she showed her father affection of any kind. I can recall how she'd reject my child while she screamed and cried. I still have those memories of how she would reject her and shove her away, each time harder than the last. The apparent cruelty and cold-heartedness of her mind games on Jai still make me tremble. I bought my daughter Jai a puppy once, a beautiful Doberman. I was so excited to take it to her and for her to meet *Bullet,* as we named him, but her mom would have none of it. We had come by for an unannounced visit to surprise her; big mistake. I remember how Jai cried and begged to see and play with the puppy, but her mother simply wouldn't allow it. On another occasion, we had bought her a beautiful canopy bed, which she loved, but once again, Esperanza turned it into manipulative ploy, telling her that if she loved that bed, she should stay in it and not come back to her. It was an unhealthy display of emotional mistreatment and all the components of suggestive reasoning in conjunction with situational vulnerability and exploitation. It was extremely painful to experience, and I was helpless to do anything about it. All I could do was reach out and put my trust in family court and my private attorney for help. Isaiah 9:17 says, "Therefore the Lord shall have no joy in their young men, neither shall have mercy on their fatherless and widows: for every one *is* an hypocrite and an evildoer, and every mouth speaketh folly. For all this his anger is not turned away, but his hand *is* stretched out still." The Bible further states in 1 John 2:1, "My little children, I am writing these things to you so that you may not sin. And if anyone sins, we have an Advocate with the Father, Jesus Christ the righteous." I felt alone and abandoned at Bronx Family Court.

MY FIGHT FOR FATHERHOOD

Parental Alienation Syndrome (PAS) is a term introduced by child psychiatrist Richard Gardner in 1985. PAS is the systematic denigration of one parent by the other with the intent of alienating the child against the other. The purpose of the alienation is usually to gain or retain custody without the involvement of the father. The alienation usually extends to the father's family and friends as well.

Dr. Richard Gardner, in his book, *The Parental Alienation Syndrome,* argues and states (P.74),

> *Many of these children proudly state that their decision to reject their fathers, is their own. They deny any contribution from their mothers. And the mothers*

often support this vehemently. In fact, the mothers will often state that they want the child to visit with the father and recognize the importance of such involvement, yet such a mother's every act indicates otherwise. Such children appreciate that, by stating the decision is their own, they assuage mother's guilt and protect her from criticism. Such professions of independent thinking are supported by the mother who will often praise these children for being the kind of people who have minds of their own and are forthright and brave enough to express overtly their opinions. Frequently, such mothers will exhort their children to tell them the truth regarding whether or not they really want to see their fathers. The child will usually appreciate that "the truth" is the profession that they hate the father and do not want to see him ever again. They thereby provide that answer–couched as "the truth"–which will protect them from their mother's anger if they were to state what they really wanted to do, which is to see their fathers. It is important for the reader to appreciate that after a period of programming the child may not know what the truth is any more and come to actually believe that the father deserves the vilification being directed against him. The end point of the brainwashing process has then been achieved.

The book also continues to share additional conducts as:
a) *The mother obstructs all attempts for you to communicate with her or the children in spite of saying 'she is not stopping the children seeing you.'*

b) *The children will suddenly start making excuses for you not seeing them. They may say they do not want gifts from you.*

> *Gifts sent will not be acknowledged, or they may even be returned–signed by the child.*

c) *Though the child supposedly doesn't want to see you, it will also suddenly stop seeing anyone connected to you. This will include close relatives, friends, etc. They will even stop talking to your neighbors and anyone who might be in direct contact with you. The mother will also stop contacting anyone connected to you in spite of outwardly claiming not to be involved in the child's attitudes. All such instances should be recorded as it is an indicator that the child is frightened rather than hateful.*

d) *The mother will pursue the strategy of obstructiveness by going to the school, clubs, and places where your children regularly visit, and state to the authorities that you are not to contact your children there.*

e) *You will find that others close to the mother will not communicate with you.*

In all, the mother's strategy will be to totally isolate the father from the children by gradually breaking every line of contact they might have with her or the children. Our enemies are not people. The Bible states in 2 Corinthians 10:3–5 that though we walk in the flesh, we do not war according to the flesh. The weapons of our warfare *are* not carnal but mighty in God for pulling down strongholds. A stronghold is a concept that a person believes and embraces, which can cause harm to himself or others. The decision to deny a father the right to have a relationship with his child is a stronghold. Every stronghold can only be broken through prayer.

On or about February 1987, we were back in family court, and I was victorious and granted visiting rights every other weekend, but Esperanza continued with her destructive behavior, apparent ruthless intentions, and no restraint. I would give her $150 dollars every week as child support money, but she lied to the court and stated I gave her nothing. I would take Jai shopping, and when her next visit came around, she would bring my daughter to me in rags and with no coat. "You have money! Buy her more stuff," she'd say. So, I decided at that point to buy Jai two of everything and explained that she could switch clothing, book bags, sneakers, and so on, but that a set must always remain at my house. At this point, it seemed as if Esperanza's treatment of me could not get worse, but there was more. Soon, she began to plant seeds and informally fabricate allegations of child abuse and neglect on my part. I recall sitting down with Ray, her husband, on several occasions and asking him why he never stepped up as a man and made his wife stop the madness. I was giving her money every week and doing my best by my child, but he simply stated, "I don't get involved in that." Of course, she'd cry in court and make baseless allegations, but thankfully, due to the lack of evidence, the court gave little credibility to what she had to say. The level of hypocrisy was overwhelming. I would pay her in five, ten, and occasionally twenty-dollar bills. She imagined the money was coming from illicit gains but simply didn't give it a second thought, and, after all, money has no conscience. On one occasion, I showed up with my new girlfriend to get Jai, and Esperanza lost her mind. She had responded by attacking us with a box cutter as if she was really a killer. She took a few swings and cut the handle of a bag I was carrying and cut my leather jacket. When I went into the bag and threatened to shoot her if she didn't back off, she chilled right away. My poor, traumatized girlfriend eventually became weary of the drama Esperanza continued to create and decided to leave me, but not before counseling me. She explained how she loved me and wanted a future with me, but my lack of formal education and "baby momma drama" was something she couldn't tolerate anymore. It was the wake-up call I needed and my personal "prodigal son" moment. I thought to myself, "My brothers are all doing well and have white-collar jobs, we come from the same gene pool, and here I am stuck, stagnant, and idle." I took it to heart and realized my girlfriend was absolutely right. A short time later, I returned to school. I got my GED (high school equivalency diploma) and a clerical training certificate and was soon on my way to bigger and better things. God was preparing my path. Isaiah 45:2–3 says, "I will go before you and will level the mountains; I will break down gates of bronze and cut through bars of iron. I will give you hidden treasures, riches stored in secret places, so that you may know that I am the LORD, the God of Israel, who summons you by name."

3
ON TOP OF THE WORLD?

At this point in my life, I had reached the ripe age of twenty-two. I went to work as a clerk in the mailroom of a fabric manufacturer under the supervision of a gentleman who happened to be Luther Vandross's brother-in-law. My job was simple—distributing and retrieving mail to the executive's inbox on his secretary's desk and posting the outgoing mail with a run to the post office at the day's end. It was an exciting new beginning, as I had gone from wearing overalls to a shirt and tie. I blended in well and decided to go a step further. I enrolled in college! The higher-ups took notice, and by God's grace, I was soon promoted to a junior executive position. It was rather funny that now I was giving orders and being serviced by who else, my former supervisor and brother-in-law to Luther V. Let's just say that I never had to remind him who was the boss. I was doing very well, but the drug dealer in me continued to emerge. Many of the young Caucasians didn't have access or the guts to travel to unsavory neighborhoods to get their drugs, so I took orders, bought them wholesale, and just like that, I was back in business, and it was booming. I had transitioned from selling marijuana to cocaine now. I would purchase half a kilo and manufacture it into a whole kilo, based on its purity.

My life was changing rapidly. I was finally on my way up financially and feeling like everything was good, but when I showed up for my weekend visits with my little girl, she was often crying and sad. "What's wrong baby? Are you alright?" I'd ask. "I'm okay, but Mommy is sad, so that makes me sad." After inquiring, I was made aware that Esperanza and Ramon/Ray were having frequent fights in front of my child, and it was affecting her emotionally. I was still single at the time and *stoned* most of the time, so I made Esperanza a proposition. I told her, "Listen, I don't like seeing my kid suffer, and I want more children. If you divorce Ray and promise to give me more children, I'll get back together with you." So, she ran to Ray and said, "Joe still loves me and wants me back." This cat hit the roof, and honestly, so did I! I mean I never said I loved her; I was trying to rescue my daughter from the madness and raucous environment she was living in, that's all! My proposition never materialized. Instead, Esperanza and Ray got back together and soon thereafter had a son, Ray Jr (little Ramon). You could say that I basically saved their marriage.

Time moved on, and I started to feel as if I was on top of the world, and I didn't seem to have any worries. I was at work when the phone rang. I answered and heard a voice say, "Mr. Rodriguez, you are needed at your residence; we can't tell you why, just come quickly." As I approached the building where I lived, the fire trucks were everywhere. I entered the building, and there was water everywhere, and the smell of smoke was thick and fresh.

I entered my apartment to find it completely covered in a black char. I entered my bedroom, and it was completely gutted and destroyed. Only the metal hangers remained in the closet, as the clothes had burned off. No mattress, just springs, and picture frames missing the pictures—it was a horrific scene. I can only compare it to a scene similar to homes after being bombed out. The windows and most of the frames were smashed out or melted away. I stood there in awe, the apartment still covered in an inch or two of water. I was living with my sister Esther and younger brother Joshua at the time, and it appeared the door to my room closed during the fire and contained the flames to my bedroom. A hole burned through the door and thus my siblings had severe smoke damage to their property, but they didn't lose much. I, on the other hand, lost it all: TV, stereo system, brass bed, my clothes. . . I was in complete and total disbelief. I drank and drank a bunch of alcohol as well as smoked excessive weed. I even did lots of blow (cocaine), but I didn't feel a thing. My mind and senses were frozen with disbelief and dismay due to the utter uncertainty and unimaginable material loss I'd just suffered. Essentially, I was in shock! A few days later, as I rode to work. I felt alone, abandoned, and in a dark, dark place. I felt shortness of breath as I thought I was thousands of feet in the hole. I got no charity, no FEMA assistance, nothing. No pity party, no pennies from anyone, and no *GoFundMe*™. My new girlfriend's mother had the grace and compassion of letting me stay in her home (just three blocks over on Pitt Street) for two weeks or so. Nevertheless, I felt so lost and alone. I was at my lowest, but I didn't want to give up sex or drugs and was angry at God, so I made a symbolic pact with the devil. I was so distraught that my thoughts were garbled. I had a silent conversation with the devil and felt God let me down. What did I have to lose, or so I thought? I couldn't understand why God would do this to me. I mean, He literally had left me with nothing but the clothes on my back. So, I told Satan, "If you help me, I'll serve you; we can get down." Out of nowhere, the White boys at work wanted heroin as well. It was the next step in elevating my drug game, seeing I was getting $3,000 for an ounce of coke compared to heroin at $8,000 an ounce; this was a no-brainer. The plan was set in motion, and I had no idea what I was really getting into. I was now in the big leagues and would soon learn it wasn't the smartest place to be at all.

It seemed the heroin I was getting was some of the purest in New York. It was over 94 percent pure, like a rock, and we had to break it up with a hammer in order to distribute the product.

Unlike the coke, I never cut or diluted these drugs in any way. Word quickly got around, but I quickly learned to only do business with a handful of selected drug distributers who would steadily buy five to six ounces every month. It was frightening to realize the product was in such high demand that I would sell out in about three to five hours. The coke didn't move as fast, but it still went out every month. After all expenses, I was making nearly $100,000 a month in the drug trade. Not bad for a struggling college student, huh? Through it all, I continued to go to school. I had left my executive position in the garment industry and was a full-time student by day and unlicensed street pharmacist by night. Now I was really feeling on top of the world, or so I thought when, in reality, I was setting up my possible destruction. I had fallen in love with the money and power. Exodus 22:20 says, "He who sacrifices to any god, other than to the Lord alone, shall be utterly destroyed."

A CLOSE CALL

The Drug Enforcement Administration had apparently caught wind of the new high-grade dope operation on the streets, and an undercover surveillance task force was formed to find those behind this and take them down. In 1984, the DEA began surveillance; they followed me, wiretapped my phone, and would go through my garbage regularly. They didn't want me; they wanted my crew and my connections and operational structure. What they didn't realize was that there was no vast operation, just one man with two associates. It was a simple operation. After purchasing a kilo, I'd have someone carry it to a certain location. I followed closely and only took control of the drugs once I reached the safehouse. When an order came in, I went to the apartment, packaged the drugs, and left them out for transport and delivery. When ordered, Mr. Flo (my runner) would collect the drugs left out for him, make the delivery, retrieve the funds, and return to the safehouse and drop the cash. The funny thing is that none of us were ever seen or photographed in public together. We avoided each other like a plague and only communicated by pager and public phones. When we needed to discuss business or exchange currency, we would make arrangements and meet at a club or a large, crowded place, somewhere really public yet exclusive. Once we identified each other, a nod was given, and we would proceed to meet in a bathroom stall. We talked business, exchanged funds, and left separately. This infuriated the federal agents because in order to prove any charge of conspiracy, they needed to film us together. They desperately needed to capture a picture or a quick shot of us, and after four years, it never happened. It seemed as though we had devised a full-proof plan. We couldn't snitch on each other for fear of full reprisal against our families and ourselves. Thinking back to my first meeting with my Jamaican connection, he put the fear of death in me without saying anything. Upon building a business rapport, I was encouraged to come by anytime, although I detested visiting. The place was full of hardcore Rastafarians, each with a loaded automatic weapon on his lap. However, after a few deals, things got comfortable, and the need for so many guns subsided. We met in underground garages, movie theaters, and, of course, nightclubs to make exchanges. Business was usually conducted outside of public view, and the exchange money was usually in my trunk and then switched to someone else's trunk and vice versa. Restaurants with valet parking were ideal; I'd sit and eat alone, we'd make eye contact, and just like that, the deal had been done. My operation had specific patterns and a solid structure that made it simple to follow but so secretive that its "ins" and "outs" couldn't be distinguished or tracked.

On the occasions that the deals were too big for me to trust Mr. Flo, I would drop off and pick up the money myself. I just had the man keep the cab running! Funny to think I trusted my guy to deliver two or three ounces of drugs and collect 24K but thought he might run away with my 40–50K. It was God's infinite mercy that protected me against being robbed, set up, or killed. Face it, when you pick up $45,000 with just a vest, a handgun, and no backup or armored car, you realize it's God's mercy that allows you to walk out and make it home alive.

I only sold bulk, so all I needed were five or six steady customers who took five to seven ounces every month, so I usually sold out in a day or two. This meant I had the rest of the month to be with my fiancée, Carmen, Jai, and attend college courses; that was my ticket out of the game. I knew one day I had to quit and go straight, and the bottom line was if I did well financially, my daughter would continue to reap the benefits.

A FAITHFUL MEETING

One night as I traveled home from school, I ran into a beautiful woman who I had not seen in a very long time and who would later become my wife. I had a routine of taking the Avenue D bus on the Lower East Side of Manhattan to First Avenue, then hopping on the "L" train for one or two stops to school in Brooklyn. It was a sweet twenty-minute commute. I had been on my way home from school on that lovely evening when I ran into her. Immediately, I felt it was fate. "Carmen, how are you? It's been a long time!" That was my initial reaction. We were both excited and continued to talk and get reacquainted. So many years had gone by since I had seen her that I couldn't resist asking her out. I couldn't stop thinking of her and felt she was exactly what I needed: a woman who was God-fearing, had a career, and was beautiful. I was afraid that this wouldn't work out, but she was the ying to my yang, the beauty who calmed this savage beast, and I didn't want to hurt her. I guess in my heart, I always knew I planned to marry a woman who knew and loved God. I knew that if one day I returned to the ways of the Lord, I would need a woman who would not bring conflict and ridicule such a decision. I know I was crazy to think this way, being a drug-dealing criminal and all, but that was the seed my parents had planted in me a long time ago.

No matter where I went or what I did, that gentle voice of conviction followed. We went to dinner and promptly fell in love. We dated for a year, lived together for another, and then got married. My wife understood that I was obtaining funds from an undisclosed source, and I simply told her my job was to provide for my family. I didn't assault people, kill people, or rob or physically hurt people. I was planning to get out of this business, but for now, I needed to continue doing some things, and I needed her to not ask me what or how. She didn't know details of my business enterprise. She didn't know if it involved gambling, heroin, cocaine, or pot. I also told her that if she was ever questioned, to say she didn't know, which, ironically, was the truth.

My heart told me she would be good for me, but I never imagined how good, valuable, and reliable she would be. In life, we all need a friend, a confidant, and a confronter. My wife of thirty-five years was and still is all these things to me and more. She has kept me on the "straight and narrow." She has drawn a line, which I've been afraid to cross, and yes, she has been a friend and trusted companion. In the good and the bad, she has been the trooper, and anyone would be proud to call her their faithful bride. Believe me, I have done it all and come close to losing it all, and in sickness and in health, she's been there. If your friends don't have the moral fiber or sense of integrity to admit certain conduct is beyond the pale, *homie, find new friends.* There needs to be a sane steady voice that you trust, value, and respect, and that's why I praise God every day for her life, love, and sacrifice.

Up until this point, I had not formally presented my daughter Jai to any of the women I dated, but this was going to be my wife, so I introduced them, and they hit it off. As you might imagine, this infuriated Esperanza, and she started withholding Jai again and resisting the court's order for visitation once more. When I reported it to the court, Esperanza's new tactic was to imply that Jai was coming into an unhealthy and abusive environment, so they essentially ordered supervised visits with a guardian present (my sister, Esther). As a result, when I picked up my daughter, my sister had to be present at all times. This inconvenience went on for about a year until my sister stated she couldn't do it anymore. She had a life of her own and couldn't be spending every other weekend with us.

My lawyer petitioned the court for change of guardianship to my wife (Carmen), and Esperanza flipped out again. "Now she is really going to be abused!" she exclaimed. "His wife will cover it up, so you know what . . . just give her to him." The judge stated that if anyone had an allegiance to me, it would likely have been my sister, as she was a blood relative and considered Carmen impartial. Additionally, Esperanza's false claim helped the judge see that she was not interested in Jennifer's safety but was simply demonstrating vindictiveness and destruction of my father-daughter relationship. One of the ludicrous things she did was question the magistrate's judgment when he made his decision by telling the judge, "Well, go ahead, then, put her in danger; give her to him."

The judge's warning did not deter her from embracing and using divisive tools. She still tried to interfere, and on one occasion, I unfortunately had to have her arrested for violating a court order. They picked her up at her job, put her in the back of a police vehicle, and delivered her to the judge. She was so unstable emotionally that I had to hide my upcoming marriage to Carmen for fear that she would not give me Jai on the weekend of the wedding.

Thankfully, we were able to celebrate our wedding and hold a beautiful reception at Victors Café 52 in New York City. Absolutely splendid! Sadly, when Esperanza found out, the tension and animosity increased. With each incident, I understood the stress of engaging anyone with a potential neurodivergent (*neurodivergent* differing in mental or neurological function from what is considered typical or normal) challenge. It was during this time that I began to realize what I believed to be cruel and evil behavior was the result of mental illness.

Once married, we started contemplating a family of our own, and I finally felt like things had subsided with my former companion. Things were good, and the court even awarded me vacation time, so I took Jai to Disney World. Sadly, my child was miserable as she had been given specific instructions to not engage or interact with us. So, it was apparently difficult for my daughter's biological mother to release her to have fun without putting more guilt trips and emotional burdens on her. I struggled with the possibility that perhaps her mother didn't want her to enjoy herself in a child's dream come true in visiting Disney World. Can you imagine any child struggling to have fun in one of the happiest places on earth? When Jennifer was about ten years old, my brother David discovered the Frederick Douglass Academy (a charter school) in Harlem, a few blocks from where she lived. Again, it was, "You are still trying to make her into a Rodriguez," and she opposed me at every step, but I managed to bribe her with several hundred dollars ($250 before and $250 after signing), and she registered Jennifer. Some criticized me for paying her off, but I was determined to make sure my daughter got an education, and Frederick Douglass was her best option. Life went on, and I was scheduled to graduate in 1989 with my associate's degree.

Me and Jennifer

Dad's Funeral

Cheyenne's High School Graduation.

The Family

4
TRIALS

One day, Mr. Flo (co-conspirator) came to me with a proposition for two to four kilos. The deal called for an exchange of hundreds of thousands, which I was strictly opposed to. However, I agreed to sell him two minus the $50,000 he gave as a deposit, and honestly, I didn't trust anyone with that amount of money or product, so I had to get involved. Mr. Flo introduced me to Frankie Cuba, and we began to negotiate. Little did I know the guy was a fed from the DEA (Drug Enforcement Agency). So I gave him an ounce so he could check out the product and began to plan for the amount of drugs ordered. He would need to collect the remaining funds and be ready to go in a day or two. It seemed we were bonding and beginning to trust one another, so then I asked the big question, "When are you going to have the rest of the money so I can deliver your product?" Frankie Cuba says: "Oh, just give me two weeks, and we'll be good to go." At that moment, my heart sank as I knew this punk was a cop. It was an easy giveaway. Most of my customers made $50,000 in a few days; so here we got a dude who claimed he could move up to four kilos but didn't have the money to close on two? We said our goodbyes and promised to meet in two weeks . . . Yeah right! I washed his $50,000 and cut all communication with him; I knew it was a setup of some sort.

Frankie Cuba called for weeks, and I stalled. I started to come up with excuses like: "I can't find it," "Nobody has anything," or "I'm looking for you; don't worry." I planned never to see him again, and then, one day, I was coming out of a McDonald's when I suddenly heard: "DEA, hands up, get against the wall!" I was handcuffed and driven to a non-descript office building on the Upper West Side of New York. I was held and questioned for hours, but they got nothing, and I lawyered up. I never gave a second thought about informing on my connections. It was simple; this was the life I chose, so if I snitched, I would last no more than a few weeks before being assassinated, so I would take my chances with the judicial system. They even arrested my wife as leverage to make me talk, but my wife knew nothing. As I stated before, I really kept nothing in my home, just a gun, a vest, and a small amount of drugs for personal use. Ironically, those agents searched my home for hours and never found any evidence. In fact, the funniest thing was that they were sitting on a couch that had a safe underneath it. It contained several grams of cocaine, cash, and, worst of all, records of customer names, transactions, and amounts. They dismantled my dropped ceiling and rummaged through clothing, the refrigerator, the whole place, and left no stone unturned, so these sophisticated "keystone" cops thought! My wife was very polite and offered them cake and coffee, made them feel at home, and told them all she knew, nothing. She told them that I put the food on the table and that she didn't know any particulars on how I did it. I protected her by insulating her the best I could, or so I thought. She was taken to DEA headquarters and booked. When I finally saw my wife at central booking, I had a brief moment to speak to her. I couldn't apologize enough, but she assured me everything was going to be fine. She was right, and even when we don't deserve it, God is working on our behalf. She was ROR (released on your own recognizance) and went home.

HARDSHIPS

In the drug game, there are only two ways out: jail or death. The most important thing in the drug game is insurance, so when you finally get busted or die, you better have your money and attorney's fees set up right since funerals and trials can be extremely expensive. My bail was a million dollars, but my lawyer was confident we could work out a defense. It was a high hill to climb as we went through boxes of evidence, but it was all circumstantial. My co-conspirators and I never spoke on our phones and only used public phones; thus, no voice recordings existed. We never spoke about drugs; a bottle of wine was an ounce; a case of champagne was code for a kilo. We used fake names and wore disguises to avoid detection. They recovered no drugs or marked money or the stash apartment, which was never located. It all seemed like a bad dream, yet my nightmare was just beginning.

Jail is like a zoo. There are people personified through the characteristics of lions, bears, wolves, crocodiles, and lambs. Lambs are eaten alive, so crocks are the way to go. A crocodile doesn't snap your face off unless you get too close or provoke it; thus, I was transformed into a person with these types of animal traits to stay alive. In life, you never know what you're capable of until you are confronted with a horrific decision and are forced to decide to live or die. I spent months in what was called Little Vietnam (Rikers Island). There were stabbings, slashings, and killings all the time. There was always blood on the walls and men getting stitched up. It was truly like a zoo with all varieties and types of animals. As for the guards, they were afraid to intervene in most altercations and would call the squad for fights they should have broken up themselves. You always heard the correction officers say, "We run this." Yeah, right! They ran what they were allowed to run, nothing more. They never had control unless we relinquished it. There were two phones in the units: one for the Blacks and one for the Hispanics. Whites got on during the day because there were no priority slots until 6:00 p.m. Seating in the TV room was also was assigned by seniority: killers in the front row with their members close behind. The reality was that the correction officers ran very little.

One time, we had so many stabbings in my unit that the squad came in one morning and turned our dorm upside down (commonly known as "a shakedown"). At the end, after everyone was stripped naked, searched, and piled into the TV room, they would leave your property in disarray, just disrespectfully piled on your bed. "Now, clean it up!" And the tough guys (corrections officers) would leave. The next day, they would come back and do it again. "Now clean it up!" Yeah right, not this time, suckers. We turned the tables on the fools and didn't clean up anything. We left the piles and mess as the morons had left it. The next morning, Sergeant. Jones, (as we called him) came in with the squad again, right on time, saw the mess, and asked, "What's going on?" Everyone replied, "&#%!@ you stupid, you clean it up this time; were not doing squat." Seriously, what could they do, put us in jail? This was the first time I saw a Black man blush. He never returned to try to pull that nonsense again. Like I said, they think they run the prison, but it's an illusion. All they control is who comes in and goes out and the lights.

My life continued to drag on as we prepared for my trial since I opted not to take the fifteen-year plea deal the feds were offering me. The madness went on day after day. Once or twice per month, they would chain me up like an animal and shackle me to another inmate so that I couldn't run. Then, they would put me on a bus and take me to a holding pen in the court building designed for about twenty guys and a one toilet (out in the open); they would put over one hundred men in this small cell for hours and hours and hours. At times, I could be caged up like that from 8:30 a.m. until 6:30 p.m. and not even see the judge. It was filthy, dangerous, and beyond uncomfortable. They called it "bullpen therapy." As stated, this went on for about one to two times each month for ten months.

One day, this punk came into the dorm and yelled out, asking who had eight o'clock on the phone. I responded it was my time, and he stated, "I'm taking it." At that point, you fought or became a chump, which would result in constant humiliation of unimaginable consequences. We wrapped our hands, prepared for the brawl, and went to the bathroom (the only place without cameras or surveillance). I pounded him, and he tried his best to pound me. The fight occurred about one hour prior to dinner, so we had time to lick our wounds and rest. I thought we had finished the matter when I heard them call, "On the chow," which was dinner. I exited the dorm and proceeded down the stairs to the mess hall. When I got to the second-floor landing, I felt a punch to the back of my head. I spun around to find the punk I had just fought with back in the dorm coming at me with a shank. I had an ice pick I enjoyed carrying because it was not as messy as the blood splatter from a slashing tool like a shank or razor. Fortunately, I had mine that day, and we both went at it, sticking and slashing all at the top of the stairs. During one exchange, I lunged and grabbed him around the waist and began to plunge the ice pick into his back, over and over until it broke in my hand. This was all taking part at the top of the stairwell, and I was trying to throw him down the steps, but he was holding on to the rail for dear life. At some point, he let go, and we both tumbled down the stairs. I ran back to my unit to find another weapon and clean the blood off me, but I was bleeding heavily from the initial slice to the back of my head. The alarm had gone off, and I was being sought, so I sat and started to pack my belongings and await an escort. I had no choice but to report to the infirmary and get ten stitches to close the wound. The nurse stated I actually had three lacerations, one near my right eye and two more lacerations to the back of the head. The punk I threw down the stairs was also there, bruised and battered, with a spike stuck in him. As the Convict Code dictates, no one tells, and no one cooperates, or you'll be subjected to be labeled a snitch (which is a death sentence in jail).

Keep in mind, prison is a cage where there is no escape. You can't run, there is nowhere to run to, and eventually, you'll wind up in a corner, face-to-face with a madman usually armed with a shank or an ox (single-edge razor). As the verse goes, "God works everything for good." After the altercation with the coward who attacked me from behind, I was moved to the Men's House of Detention (The Tombs) in Manhattan. I never wondered what happened to that guy and knew if we ever crossed paths again, I would probably kill him. Next thing you know, I was at the Tombs, where I continued to prepare for the trial of my life.

TRIBULATIONS

Believe it or not, this was all a blessing and, of course, part of God's plan. As the Bible states in Romans 8:28, "We know that God works all things together for good for the ones who love God, for those who are called according to his purpose." The Tombs facility was quite different. Rikers was a dump, nasty and dirty, and even the Cos were nasty and dirty. At the Tombs, I had my own cell, and best of all, the mad, disgusting process they put the visitors through was no more. No more bus rides across the bridge to a processing area and then another bus ride to the facility, and no more "frisk and search" before a family member saw their loved ones. All my honey had to do now was enter the building and take an elevator upstairs.

One day, my wife, Carmen, brought my parents to see me, and my heart broke in a million pieces when my father began to cry. Then Momma started crying and stated, "Your father promised he wouldn't cry." I truly felt a deep pain that penetrated my heart profoundly. I grabbed their hands and promised them that they would never see me again in this situation. My mother prayed with me often over the phone and, one day, told me as I prepared for trial: "Tell them it wasn't you. You are a new creation in Christ; therefore, that was not you; that man has died." That's the love of a mother. No matter how many people I may have killed or poisoned through my destructive enterprise, no matter how many lives I ruined or criminal acts I was responsible for causing, I was still her innocent baby boy. It's ironic how I had to go to jail for God to get my attention and reclaim me as His own. Late one night, as I poured out my heart to God to deliver me, the Holy Spirit descended into my cell and fell upon me. I began to speak in tongues and shake and shiver uncontrollably. Acts 4:31 says, "And when they had prayed, the place where they had gathered together was shaken, and they were all filled with the Holy Spirit and began to speak the word of God with boldness." 1 Corinthians 2:4 says, "And my message and my preaching were not in persuasive words of wisdom, but in demonstration of the Spirit and of power." It was then that I knew my God was real and totally in control of my life and future. I felt a new sense of peace and confidence that I should go to trial and not admit to anything.

My trial began in October 1990, and ironically, I was forced to share court time with the Teflon Don. It just so happened that John Gotti was also on trial before the same judge, Edward J. Mclaughlin. The prosecutor had offered me fifteen years if I pleaded guilty on all counts, which included conspiracy and RICO (Racketeering, Influence, Corruption, Organization) statutes, but I refused. Next, the attorneys were all successful in having our cases separated, so my three co-conspirators and I went to trial individually. The federal witness (DEA agent) stated I was running a criminal enterprise and was conspiring in the trafficking and distribution of heroin and cocaine supplied by Jamaican and Asian connections in New York. He stated I was part of a criminal enterprise that may have even been involved in murders, extortions, and money laundering.

The feds seriously attempted to paint me as a cold-blooded criminal with the ability to obtain the purest heroin and cocaine they had ever seen. But as the State's witness was crossed-examined, his perception had no foundation or basis. In fact, all the allegations and theories fell flat with the exception of the ounce of dope I gave him in advance. He tried to connect and persuade the jury that my words were codes with hidden meanings, but he couldn't clearly connect the dots. The problem was that we used codes for everything. We didn't use our actual legal names. In regards to the conspiracy charges, they had followed me for over three years and didn't have one single picture of me with any associates or known criminal figures. There is no denying that I was involved in crime. There is no denying that I did terrible things that I will forever regret. There is and will always be a code; business is business, and if that is what you have chosen, there can be no regrets because everyone knows the rules.

To this day, I feel remorse for the lives I ruined, stole, and destroyed, but regret will not change or restore anyone or anything. Would I change anything? Would I have refused the cup? I did what I did and paid as God has seen fit. As for the witness, he really couldn't convince the jury of his far-reaching allegations and claims, and the evidence was quite weak to support. I was compelled to take the stand, but my attorney advised me against it. Instead, we called my younger brother Joshua, who was a youth pastor at the time, as a character witness. My attorney was able to use him to paint a picture of my upbringing without the need for me to take the stand.

"Tell us, Joshua, do you attend school?" "And your brother, does he attend as well?" "What church do you attend, and does your brother visit as well?" This went on for some time, and in my heart of hearts, after Josh testified, the jury was not looking at me the same way. He had helped to humanize me in front of the jury, and I felt a sense of peace when he concluded. The jury deliberated for several hours and then rendered their verdict of *Not Guilty* on conspiracy to run a criminal enterprise, *Not Guilty* on conspiracy to launder money, *Not Guilty* on conspiracy to distribute, and *Not Guilty* on any violation of RICO statutes. Then, the final count: *"Guilty of sale of a controlled substance"*; the ounce I had given to the "snitch!" I was remanded, chained up, and sent back to my cell. It bears mentioning that I had given my heart to the Lord several months prior to this, and I was confident that God was going to do something.

I had prayed and asked God for direction. I even received the gift of the Holy Spirit while fervently praying one night. I felt led to go to trial. Sure enough, God's ways are not our ways, but He knows what we need. When it came time for sentencing, the heroin had been stupidly kept in a warm area, and some of it had evaporated over time; therefore, the weight of the drugs would have a direct reflection on my sentence. Shockingly, in 1990, the sentence for the sale of one ounce or more was a minimum of fifteen years to life; the sale of less than an ounce was a maximum sentence of eight years to life. The material evidence had evaporated. I believe it was a combination of the judge's anger of Gotti beating another case and God's grace of removing some of the content in the evidence bag that motivated him to sentence me to seven years to life. It was truly a miracle because I'm positive that when I gave the drugs to the undercover agent, it was a full ounce. I know it sounds crazy, but I believe that God was working behind the scenes while I prayed and asked for forgiveness, intervention, and mercy. This was the driving force that made a way for the charge to drop from a *Class A1* felony to a *Class A2* felony, which carried eight years to life maximum. I didn't have a record, and the judge could have given me two or three years, but instead, he decided to make me part of the new mass incarceration movement, which was established in 1980 and continued until 2004 until the drug law was reformed. If I were sentenced today under the newly revised law as a non-violent first offender, I'd probably be sentenced to a six-month shock program/prison boot camp.

5

AN HONEST ATTEMPT TO LIVE WELL

I was in a haze; it didn't feel real—seven years to life. It sounded like a life sentence that I may never come home from, but at that moment in time, I was simply a number, a misfit con who was being thrown into a cage for the protection of society.

God knows everything, and His timing is perfect. I arrived at the reception area at Downstate Correctional Facility (121 Red Schoolhouse Road, Fishkill, NY). After you are shaven clean of all hair and "de-liced," you are given some brief orientation and classified. However, when they discovered I had a college degree and was bilingual, they decided to keep me at *Downstate* and make me a bilingual substance abuse counselor for a whopping salary of six dollars a day. I simply gave a class to the consistently changing and ever-flowing parade of inmates that flowed through and were processed daily. I remained at *Downstate* Correctional for about three years. The prison also had college courses accredited by Marist College, so I immediately signed up. I was enrolled in a paralegal and criminal justice certification course and BS in psychology.

I spent a lot of time in the law library, researching and working on my appeal as well as helping other men with motions, petitions, and addressing civil rights violations. God blessed me with insight and gifts in this subject matter to the extent that I was able to do legal work for a fee. Payments for my assistance were made to an outside PO box. After payment was confirmed, paperwork was released to the customer. I made out very well, making hundreds of dollars a month doing legal work while working toward my degree. During my time there, the Department of Corrections created a hub system, which essentially took the map of New York and cut it into four pieces. The objective was simple. For example, after you had the classification as a maximum (six years and above) security inmate, if you landed in, say, Attica (which is seven to eight hours away) and as you completed time, your classification kept dropping to medium or minimum status, and as your time or sentence became shorter, you would then be transferred to a prison near Attica (the region where you began your time) instead of being moved all over the state. Until this day, I don't know why, but I kept the map and other supporting documents related to this new policy. Only God knew why.

One day, I had some words with a female civilian employee who I later found out happened to be having an affair with the warden. For some reason, she had wanted me to work for her, compiling rolls. A roll was a blanket, sheet, pillowcase, two pants, two shirts, a jacket, socks, toothbrush, and toothpaste, all rolled up in a single "roll." The woman apparently didn't like me. On one occasion, I received a day off for getting a wisdom tooth pulled, and she went bananas. When I received another day off for getting the other wisdom tooth pulled out, she fired me. Next thing you know, I was on my way to Watertown, New York, just thirty-five miles from the St. Lawrence River in Canada (an extremely racist part of the state). The voyage of transporting someone is simple. First, you are chained and shackled around the waist, attached to that is a pair of handcuffs, and then you are chained to another person at the ankle; thus, if you run, he has to run with you. We stopped at a century-old prison called Auburn; that was the halfway point. Auburn was founded in 1818, and it appeared nothing had been upgraded; even the sound of the clang when the bars shut closed sounded authentic. We slept overnight in cells until we were transported the remainder of the way. I arrived in October '93 and immediately began to devise a plan to get out of one of the most racist places I had ever seen. Not one single black guard in the whole place, and the manner in which they treated the inmates was despicable. Strangely, the knucklehead guards didn't mess with me. God's grace was upon me, and my reputation as a savvy and skilled litigator had preceded me. I had taken on the Supreme Court judge who sentenced me, the DEA, the Federal Court, and one of New York's top prosecuting attorneys and won time after time. Additionally, since I worked as a paralegal in the Law Library, I had assisted countless men with appeals, motions, and petitions of all types, and I became very familiar with processes, laws, and rights violations.

However, at the present moment, I was in Gouverneur Correctional Facility, "Last Stop in America." We inmates referred to it as such because it was so far out and so close to Canada that if you spat through the fence, it would land in Canada. I immediately began to compile my petition to be transferred to a facility close to the one I had just been transferred from and was met by resistance after resistance. It was kind of a joke if you think about it: *little ol' me was gonna take on the New York State Department of Corrections from behind bars with no co-counsel.* No one thought I stood a chance, especially "Woo." After getting settled, I met an Asian gentleman with thick glasses and a prosthetic leg named Woo. He would tell me that if he couldn't get moved for hardship reasons, I had less of a chance. The man left me thinking, and I sensed he was right in one aspect; I had no real, valid hardship. Therefore, I decided to attack them on procedural grounds of violating their very own new rules, policies, and procedures that dictated and approved transfers. I had exhibits that explained and detailed the HUB system and how it was supposed to work. I articulated how they violated its policies and my rights to be treated fairly and justly, based on their own policies. My poor wife had made the painful journey (some twelve hours) to come see me. She endured the ride and visited me twice, and I told her not to return as I would be leaving soon. Matthew 9:29 says, "Then He touched their eyes, saying, according to your faith let it be to you." God was activating my faith, and by January 1994, I was on my way back toward New York/Fishkill, New York. You see, one of my areas of focus in my petition against The Dept. of Corrections stated that my college education had been interrupted, and it was the vehicle to my rehabilitation. Another point was that college degrees for incarcerated inmates had been done away with a few months prior, but the Marist College administrators stated that anyone already enrolled in their program at the time would be grandfathered in and allowed to finish their degrees. I even stated that if they wanted to send me even farther into Canada, I would happily go as long as they had a Marist College program. All the while, I knew the only medium security-level facility that had such a program was Fishkill Correctional Facility, just minutes from Downstate Correctional, the prison they had moved me from. What an awesome experience, which, once again, clearly demonstrates God's protection and support. The Bible states in 1 John 4:4, "Greater is he that is in you, than he that is in the world." I had only spent three to four months at Watertown when I was packed up and transferred back down toward New York once more. Where do you wonder to? To Fishkill, of course. I arrived at Fishkill and began settling in. Fishkill was old and falling apart, but as God would have it, there was a blessing awaiting me there. As I was applying to continue my studies, I was tipped off to special housing for inmates attending college. Matthew 7:7 says, "Ask and you shall receive, seek and you shall find knock and" [boom] "it shall be opened to you." Can you say honor dorm? It was so quiet, clean, and orderly. When you arrived, you were placed in a dormitory setting. There were about twenty private cells, and as you arrived, you were placed on a waiting list. single cells, college, and the best food to come out of a can! Everyone thought I was fine, but inside, I was so deeply sad! Even though I had plenty of money, and my beautiful wife sent me all the food items (up to thirty-five pounds per month) I requested, I was still depressed and miserable.

Prison is designed for one thing and one thing only: extreme deprivation; deprived of your freedom, favorite food, contacts with friends, family, and children; deprived of smelling fresh cut grass, the beach, and the sound of the surf; and deprived of going to the bodega or the Chinese restaurant. At night, when all is quiet, it really hits you. For those without financial support and an extremely strong sense of survival, you won't last. I had fallen asleep on countless nights, praying to God to take me. I asked Him to allow me to die in my sleep. I pleaded with Him to end the madness, to stop the pain, but each day I would wake up, and it was Groundhog Day again. You see, in prison, there are no days of the week. Every day, it's the same thing; same people, same routine, and the same process of being counted several times per day. In addition, some corrections officers attempt to humiliate you with degrading comments and just plain stupidity because they attempt to hide behind a tin badge. I recall one such corrections officer commenting and ridiculing some inmates who were worshiping Jesus, "They used to sell crack in the streets, but now want to serve Christ because they're in jail." The guy was the typical example of the insensitive, condescending, abusive, and dehumanizing corrections officers we dealt with regularly. He refused to see the change in a man when he had a personal encounter with Christ, but we know the devil will use anything and anyone to try to wound and discourage God's people.

The years passed slowly, one, two, three, four, five, six, seven years. *"Why my Lord? When shall it end . . . My God, why have you turned away? Why have you forgotten me? Shall you never answer my prayers?"* I tried to keep as busy as I could, studying, reading, and simply praying and meditating on God's Word. At times, it felt hopeless, but I was reminded that life is a marathon and not a race, so I had to hold on and continue to embrace Philippians 4:7, which says that God gives us "peace that surpasses all understanding." My wife would come visit me regularly, every other week. I was only about two hours from home, so it wasn't a long trip for her, but I wanted to be compassionate and give her time to live as well. I encouraged her to go out with her friends and family. She even went on a cruise with her sisters and friends. I told her not to feel guilty as I was the one locked up, not her.

My family suffered along with me. They would come see me periodically and would write often. My wife would bring Jai up every other week. We had such a great relationship at times. Jai and I would write (snail mail) each other often. In fact, I've kept the letters. Poor kid. Carmen was always there as Esperanza battled a bad marriage and an apparent emotional breakdown that put her in the hospital until she was stabilized and assessed to not be a danger to herself and others. God helped to deliver and subsequently discharge her in His time, while I still awaited my long and protracted exit.

One week was a visit with Carmen, and the other with my daughter. It was a good arrangement, and since Carmen was giving Esperanza money to help with my daughter, she didn't mind allowing her stepmother to bring her up to see me. Additionally, my family always attempted to include Jai's mother in events, so she would not experience a single scintilla of jealousy and help her financially when she was in need. They would pacify Cookie by inviting her to weddings and allowing her to take group photos with the Rodriguez family. They really tried to help in the areas of inclusion so we could all get along. Jai would write me great letters. She was inspired and proud that I was getting my bachelor's degree as well as criminal justice and paralegal certifications. My daughter was also in a college prep course that gave her college credits for taking classes at Columbia and living on campus during the summer. Her stepmom Carmen had helped move her in and brought her all she needed.

While I was still away, Esperanza continued to have struggles with her current spouse, Ray. I had been informed of major disputes that had led to a separation. Her mental state appeared fragile, and thankfully, she sought help. I prayed for her and hoped that I would not be used as a scapegoat in the midst of the apparent hell that she was experiencing in her personal life. I hoped that she would not use her pain and frustration to further debilitate my relationship with my daughter Jai.

God continued to work on my behalf within the prison walls. Soon, I hit the six-year mark and requested an early release. I had done all I could in terms of programs. I had obtained a Bachelor of Science degree, a criminal justice certification, a paralegal certification, and had accumulated good behavior days; you would think I had done enough! Ironically, it turned out that the state had implemented a new program called CASAT (Comprehensive Alcohol Substance Abuse Treatment) that no one was attending. The Department of Corrections decided that in order to fill the program, they would deny release to anyone who had a drug crime. It didn't matter if you used or sold drugs, if you didn't attend their cheesy program, you weren't going home. What could I do? I was essentially blackmailed, so I signed up. I could now actually see the end of the tunnel. It took a few weeks to finally transport me. I did my six months of CASAT, and finally, on April 28, 1995, after six years and seven months, I was placed in a work-release program and sent home with the stipulation of finding employment in ninety days.

Free at last, free at last! Thank God Almighty, I was free at last. Hold it! Not so fast; remember, I had a life sentence. I had learned the valuable meaning of surviving in the jungle/in the belly of the beast. I thought I had defeated the darkness, but it had taken a hold within me. The years I spent behind the wall had made me bitter, and the thoughts of revenge were a constant companion. Not long after I came home, I ran into a guy who owed me money and expected to be forgiven. I grabbed him and threatened to either cut off an ear or a finger if he didn't pay me, and news alert, we both knew I wasn't kidding. Fortunately, the guy paid me, and I wasn't challenged to make good on my threat, but I encountered an ugly and disturbing side of me I didn't realize still existed. The feeling tormented me, and I felt torn between my manhood and my faith. The Bible recounts in Luke 22:49–51, "When Jesus' followers saw what was going to happen, they said, "Lord, should we strike with our swords?" And one of them struck the servant of the high priest, cutting off his right ear." My heart was heavy as I understood how Peter lost it for a moment. I had to continue to practice sacrificing and kill that old man, die to self daily, and more of letting Christ to take hold and live within me. Galatians 2:20 says, "I am crucified with Christ: nevertheless I live; yet not I, but Christ liveth in me: and the life which I now live in the flesh I live by the faith of the Son of God, who loved me, and gave himself for me."

6

REINTEGRATION

The way the reentry system works is that upon your release, you are given twelve weeks to find a job. It's not as easy as it sounds. The state puts you in this program, which requires you to participate in community service two days a week, in most cases, in rat-infested, neglected, and impoverished neighborhoods. I recall working as a janitor's helper in the Bronx. I was supposed to assist this guy out in the garbage shoot room in the basement of the building. The large rats would run along the plumbing as if it was a highway just above where we were working. These nasty vermin would run around in broad daylight, hundreds of them, well aware that they were beyond our reach. It was troubling to see how they hung out in bunches and observed us. This served as a huge motivator to get another job and get out of this literal rathole. My plan consisted of researching and sending out resumes and planning interviews one day a week. I did my disgusting community service for two days and went on interviews the remaining two days of the week. My interview skills needed to be sharp since I had to discreetly cover the seven years that I was away and out of the work force. I simply stated the truth. I stated that I was a substance abuse counselor at Fishkill Correctional Facility and was attending Marist College at night. I simply left out the part about living at the Fishkill Correctional Facility. As I searched for work, I was interviewed by an exceptional and compassionate woman who looked beyond my one and only contact with the authorities and gave me a position as an after-care worker. This job entailed preparing youth who were aging out of foster care. God surely demonstrated His goodness and mercy through this process. God is so worthy to be praised!

STRUGGLE AMIDST GROWTH

In September 1996, Carmen and I experienced a miracle. After many years of praying and trying to get pregnant, it finally happened. We were pregnant and expecting a child. On June 13th, 1997, my wife went into labor, and the next morning, a beautiful little girl named Cheyenne Lynn entered the world. We continued to pray and ask God for a breakthrough in reaching my oldest daughter Jai, but she appeared to be fearful of contact. Perhaps she was afraid to get to know her sister and fall in love with her and the family! She was fearful, for most assuredly, this could have been perceived as a betrayal of her biological mother. Jai visited us and saw her little sister Cheyenne shortly after she was born and, unfortunately, never returned to visit her little sister again for a long time. Life went on, and God steadily poured out blessing upon blessing, even though I was not fully committed to serving God in spirit and in truth. Life was good, or so I thought. My attitude has always been that three years at a job is plenty. When you've peaked and can't advance any further, it's time to go!

I landed a new job in the field of social services that did not involve working directly with children anymore. I had seen my share of abused and neglected children and no longer wanted that type of a job. All was well with me, and suddenly, I felt as though Satan came knocking on my door. After Esperanza finalized her divorce with Ray, it seemed she had remarried, this time, to a cop. I had been at my new position for about two weeks when this short cop in plain clothes came into my office, accompanied by two other uniformed cops. The little guy, Esperanza's new husband (Joseppi C), said, "I have something for you," to which I replied, "If it's not a warrant, you are trespassing without just cause." I demanded that they get out of my office and get announced by security and indicated that if I desired to answer my phone, I might allow them permission to come up. I then proceeded to call 911 since these irresponsible individuals were not there on official business and, in my view, were trespassers. They ran out at that point, but not before I obtained the badge number of one of the cops. Later, an official police officer responded when I called 911, and I filed a report. I described how this police officer had apparently stalked and tracked me down using police department data. He had evidently used official equipment and municipal resources to personally assist his wife in a personal family court matter out of his jurisdiction. I also reported that he bypassed and evaded security in my workplace under the guise and false pretense of official police business.

After internal affairs got involved and strongly reprimanded him, he left me alone and never engaged me in any manner. The magnitude of disciplinary action was so severe that it prompted internal affairs to contact me when he requested a transfer. They requested my opinion on his mental status and asked if I had incurred any additional problems since the filing of my formal complaint. I stated that I had no objections and felt that he had respected my privacy and maintained healthy boundaries after their thorough investigation into his unethical, unprofessional, and unlawful actions.

In the United States of America, many unconventional mothers believe that children do not need any type of interaction or relationship with their biological fathers. Research has demonstrated that the absence of a biological father in the life of children leads to all types of dysfunctions and destructive behaviors. Our broken judicial system places an emphasis on financial support but neglects the importance of the relationship between the bio-logical father and the child. During this difficult season in my life, the court system demanded that I pay child support for my oldest daughter while allowing, essentially, no interaction between her and me. They had moved and not disclosed an address or phone number; thus, contact had been cut off once again, this time lasting about five years.

My beautiful wife Carmen continued to pray and would tell me to leave this stressful situation to God. One day, out of the blue, I was served with the request for an increase in child support, so I made my way down to the Bronx family court. When the case was called, the judge asked me if I was opposed to the increase. I responded by saying that I was being asked to support a child I had not seen for at least five years. I had no knowledge if she was in school, married, alive, or dead. The judge agreed with me and ordered Esperanza ensure that my daughter be physically present at the next court appearance. About two months later, we were back in court, and when I saw my now nineteen-year-old daughter in the waiting area, she didn't even look at me, even though we were sitting directly in front of each other. I tried to speak to her, but she refused to speak. I persisted and, at one point, requested that Esperanza grant her permission to speak. Finally, she said something. "I'm fine," she exclaimed. I asked, "How's school?" She said, "It's fine." That's all she was allowed to say or did say. At one point, I commented that she was being stubborn, just like when she was a little girl and I was teaching her how to ride a bike, but she hung in there. All of a sudden, she replied, "You didn't teach me how to ride a bike. Mom did." At that point, I truly understood how seriously confused my daughter was. Once inside, the judge asked me if I was satisfied, and I stated I was but that I had not been allowed to contact or interact with my daughter in over five years and shared that if counseling could be requested, I would pay the requested increase. Esperanza objected, and the judge denied my request for counseling. The child support payments continued to be withheld from my salary and were sent to her just as usual. I was more than happy to financially provide for my daughter. She is my child, and by the court withholding the funds and paying them out, I did not have to keep records of payments, and the documentation would prove that I always provided for my child despite fictitious rumors that contradicted that reality.

I continued working diligently and building on my skills and knowledge of the social service industry. I was soon promoted to case manager in Preventive Care (this avoided children from being placed within the system). I worked at United Families of East Harlem and saw my daughter as often as possible. I remember Esperanza always making the comment, "Treat my daughter well, as she may be the only child you ever have." Negativity was never given a place in our lives, and when Jai graduated from Frederick Douglass High School in 1997, I was there with my beautiful pregnant wife to bless and celebrate her. Carmen's pregnancy was a miracle that surprised many. Esperanza was not thrilled with the news and suggested that our daughter Jai did not need any more siblings.

Throughout the years, I continued to have tension with Esperanza and did my best to communicate that I would continue to support my daughter despite her resistance to my visitation rights. I prayed and prayed, and within a few weeks, I was in court again, asking the judge to order therapy and enforce the previous order. My attorney pleaded with the court and outlined her apparent use of PAS (parental alienation syndrome) to control and manipulate my daughter. By now, the judge was frustrated (as the case went back over ten years at that point) and stated that Jai was old enough (sixteen) to see me if she wished, so he refused to grant my visitation request at this time. That day, I learned that racism, classism, and discrimination still take on many forms. I stood there a Black Latino, convicted felon against a woman and her White Italian cop husband (Jossepi C.). I never stood a chance in the *"us (Whites) versus them (Blacks)"* racist mindset. God may not give us what we ask for, but He'll certainly give us what we need; thus, I decided to wait upon the Lord.

Life continued and was going well. Our beautiful baby girl was born, and we now had a home in New Jersey. Cheyenne was in private school, and the Lord continued to restore many years of losses. We had pictures of Jai all around our home, and in order to protect Cheyenne, we would always tell her that Jai was one of her cousins. We hated to lie to her, but what were we going to say? We refused to tell her that Jai was her sister, apparently suffered from PAS, and that Jai's mother had misinformed, manipulated, and confused her. My wife, however, couldn't withhold the truth anymore, and when Cheyenne was five years old, she informed her that she had an older sister. All my little girl could say was, "I have a sister? Do I really have a sister?" "Yes baby, we didn't know how to tell you." That year, we had my sister Esther reach out to Jai since she still was not taking my phone calls. She received my money but not my calls. Coincidentally, Jai had turned twenty-one that year as well, and child support was discontinued. Cheyenne's birthday was being planned, and the Power Puff Girls were expected to make an appearance. My sister, Esther, successfully convinced Jai to attend Cheyenne's party, and she appeared to want to get to know her sister and bond with her. As the night was winding down, Jai whispered to me that she needed to talk to me. I told her to call me, and we could have lunch. A few days later, we met for lunch, and she stated that things were well and she was returning home from college. Then she got to her ulterior motive, "I need $3,000 to get an apartment, for security deposit, first month's rent, and a little furniture." She went on to say that she had a roommate who she knew and trusted. I told her that we had an extra bedroom, and she could live with us while she saved money. "No, I don't think so," she replied. I stated that it was not smart to have a roommate as she might move out and leave her holding the bag. "Oh no, that won't happen. I know her. If you don't want to give me the money, that's fine." I responded, "You're my daughter, and I've always supported you, so I'll give you the money, but I'm telling you it's not a wise move." I gave her the money she requested and within three months, ring-ring. "Dad, it's me. My roommate left me stranded and moved in with her boyfriend. I found another apartment, but I need $200 for an application fee." And just like that, she abandoned our relationship, alienated her sister, and withdrew from the entire Rodriguez family for another five years. As you could imagine, this was very painful for all of us, but we continued to offer olive branches along the difficult journey and continued to pray and wait on God.

HOPE OVER DISAPPOINTMENT

Slowly, I began to attend a congregation and submitted to the lead pastors at Cityline Church in Jersey City, New Jersey. God continued to open my mind and my heart. Then, it happened! I took discipleship courses and joined a group of men who were getting the congregation's prison ministry off the ground. It began slowly with just four men. It grew and grew to the point where we had twelve men and six women who could now start to service the female population at the Hudson Correctional Facility in New Jersey. Some might find it strange that after spending seven years in the belly of the beast (prison) that I would ever imagine volunteering to go back willingly, but that is exactly what I did. It is humbling to see these men and women in their surroundings and have the honor to speak into their lives. Matthew 25:36 says, "I needed clothes, and you clothed me, I was sick and you looked after me, I was in prison and you came to visit me." My pastor and younger brother, Bishop Dr. Joshua Rodriguez, always teaches us that one word from God can change a person's life. As we minister to the prison population, we always pray that God would prepare the hearts of those we would come into contact with. We also believe that one life can change the world. A clear example of this is that of the late Pastor David Wilkerson. He was used by God to witness to the world renown Evangelist Nicky Cruz. After getting saved,

Nicky went on to work for and further develop Teen Challenge International all over the globe, a mega ministry dedicated to rehabilitating men and women coming out of the prison system and men suffering from substance abuse. Nicky has been able to reach hundreds of thousands of people globally who, in turn, have been able to reach multitudes themselves. Nicky is proof God can and will use anyone to fulfill His plan and divine purpose. Not surprisingly, Nicky continues to reach men and women coming out of the prison system globally until today.

I once heard a pastor compare prison to hell. "It's a bad place where they put bad people." Their families know that they are in this bad place because they committed bad acts, so they are housed together and commit atrocities on each other, too horrific to imagine. It takes something special to do what God calls us to do, to enter these dangerous housing units, speak into an inmate's life, and ignore the heinous crimes that got them there. We don't really care about their past, for it is God who will judge them and determine where they will spend eternity. It's difficult to hold the hand of someone accused of a double homicide or a pedophile and pray for them, asking God to intervene and break through the darkness and despair that has brought this person to this place, yet this is what we have been called to do. During more than fifteen years of service in the prison ministry, I've contemplated quitting, but I always hear a voice that says, "You were created for a time such as this. If not you, then who?"

We serve a God who never fails, and He continued to work in my life and prosper me. I continued to work harder and was able to strengthen my skillset in mental health awareness. Within a relatively short period of time, I acquired a position as a director of a housing program for SPEMI (Severely, Persistently, Emotionally, Mentally, Ill). It was challenging to deal with this particular segment of the population, but with God's help, I was able to take a dwindling program that was collapsing and convert it into a viable, vital, and functioning program that's still running today. I loved it. The office was on 149th Street, so I just had to cross the George Washington Bridge from New Jersey into New York City, and I was there. During this wonderful time in my life, I had purchased a crouch rocket aka sport bike (2000 Suzuki GSXR), which I absolutely loved to ride on. I wore all the right gear and was ready for pretty much anything. As I left my office on a beautiful sunny day, I hit a crater-type pothole, which had been created by a salt spreader and remained there due to the negligence of Con Edison in New York City. I was ejected, and POW! I shattered my right knee. The patella broke into several pieces, and my surgeon did his best to save the biggest pieces and fuse them together. About a year later, the pain was unbearable, and the rest of the patella was removed. It looked deformed and hideous. I will share this incident in detail further along in the next chapter, but this particular accident would definitely throw me for a loop in many ways. Sometimes God takes drastic measures to get our attention, and when He does, it's best to listen attentively. I had seen God's fidelity throughout my life before, and this wouldn't be an exception.

7
LIVING WELL BUT WITHOUT RESOLUTION

While all these events were happening in my life, my daughter Jai was still estranged from our family. Jai continued on with her life and was still withdrawn. She had several children of her own and, unfortunately, has used the unresolved issues of the past to serve as a vehicle of alienation and withdrawal. I see now how naïve I was to assume that Jai would bond with her stepsister and grow together as a blended family. In reality, that did not happen. Our adversary Satan is in the business of dividing and splitting families. At times, deep pain and wounds can create feelings of rejection and result in the discarding of sacred relationships. This can create confusion, hate, and resentment. I have to fight against these feelings every day of my life and ask God to help me keep my heart pure. As a grandfather who has been alienated from his grandkids, I must continue to lean on God for comfort and peace. My youngest daughter has also suffered the blows of rejection for things that she is not responsible for. Regardless, we have stood firm on God's Word. The book of Joshua 1:9 says, "Be strong and courageous. Do not be afraid or terrified because of them, for the LORD your God goes with you; he will never leave you nor forsake you." There comes a time when you hear God's answer to a prayer, though it was not the answer you expected.

As I waited on God throughout the years, I had a few health scares and decided to create a will, which included an inheritance for my grandchildren. I set aside an amount for each of my grandchildren, even though they had been alienated from us. In 2016, I had sent Jai a check and a portrait of her sister's graduation. From what I was told, upon receiving the gifts, she destroyed the check and cursed out the poor brother who had delivered them. This was a very sad moment. We had sent those things in love, yet she cursed and rejected them. Every relationship should be rooted in love and never based on what you can get. For years, I tried calling and texting, never getting a reply until, one day, God said, "Give it to me." "Cast all your cares upon me." For years, I had held on to hope, miserable at times but believing God would fill the void.

That decision of rejecting the gift of love and connection to family boggles the mind. In life, you should desire more people to love your child, more people to care for, and, of course, more people to bless and pray for your child, not less. That act of rejection cut deep; the selfishness was chilling. Richard Gardner's concept of parental alienation syndrome (PAS) is real. At times, for reasons that we may never understand, it is possible for a person to have his rights denied. The minds of children can be manipulated, and they can be deceived. They can be led to a place of division and alienation.

Dealing with all of this took a physical, spiritual, and emotional toll on me as well. At times, the pain was extreme, and my mind would start to race. "Don't look back," the Lord commanded of Lot's wife, but she couldn't resist the temptation. The story of Lot and his wife is found in Genesis 19. God had determined to destroy Sodom and Gomorrah for their wickedness

(Gen. 18:16–33), and two angels warned Abraham's nephew Lot to evacuate the city so he and his family would not be destroyed. In Genesis 19, it says, "The two [angels in the form of] men said to Lot, 'Do you have anyone else here—sons-in-law, sons or daughters, or anyone else in the city who belongs to you? Get them out of here, because we are going to destroy this place. The outcry to the LORD against its people is so great that He has sent us to destroy it.'" As the family fled, "the Lord rained down burning sulfur on Sodom and Gomorrah, from the Lord out of the heavens" (Gen. 19:24). But then, in disobedience to the angel's command, "Lot's wife looked back, and she became a pillar of salt." I also failed the test of temptation and looked back. The pain and mental anguish was too severe for me. I had too much stress and too much money. Suddenly, I found myself stoned, wired, and woozy, for the relapse had occurred. I had begun to self-medicate once more during a weak point in my life. Before I knew it, I was doing $3,000 worth of coke per month. I did about one to two grams of coke each night and washed it down with either Chivas or Johnny Black Scotch. It was tragically sad. I would start getting high at 8 p.m. and keep going until 3–4 a.m. It was utter madness. I had hit a new kind of bottom, a new dark place, one of my own making. This time, my excessive personality and destructive addiction was truly going to cost me everything. My wife would find me passed out on the sofa with the TV going night after night until she felt the health risks or agony of watching me kill myself couldn't be ignored any longer. "I'm going to leave you, Joel, unless you get help." That cocaine had a hold on me, and I still had a bunch. My world seemed like it was crashing down around me. I struggled with my thoughts and how addiction had a hold on my life. One Sunday morning in December 2002, my wife and Cheyenne left for church, and something came over me as I was alone with God and my thoughts. I was at my wits' end. I fell on my knees and face and began to cry out to God. I asked him to take this addiction away from me and grant me the peace that surpasses all understanding. When

I got up from the floor, I got all the drugs I had and flushed them. Strangely, I felt liberated at that very moment. I had to see my addiction for what it was, a demon—a demon that took hold and wanted to rob me of my wife, child, home, and all else; for what? A quick sniff of powder? It was clear that it was a demon I needed to eradicate and would never let back into my life. It was a breakup of dramatic proportions. It wasn't easy, but it was worth it. In fact, until this very day, I hear the word cocaine, and it frightens me. Our pastor tells us that sometimes we have to run, not walk away from temptation; I got one better" simply follow three of the core beliefs of AA and NA, which plainly states people, places, and things. I surrounded myself with good, clean, God-fearing people. I don't visit drug spots nor hang in bars, and I've grabbed ahold of God's promises. Jeremiah 30:8 says, "'It shall come about on that day,' declares the Lord of hosts, 'that I will break his yoke from off their neck and will tear off their bonds; and strangers will no longer make them their slaves.'"

THE DEVIL MAY TRY

When I think back throughout the years, I realize now that the devil has been trying to kill me for a long time. When I was very young, my dad was taking care of us while Mom was away. I had a tricycle and wanted to shoot down the hill like my brothers were doing; only thing was they had a two-wheeler with brakes. At the bottom of the hill was the FDR Drive southbound lane. All that separated the two was about twenty feet of rod iron fence. I came down that hill, and my little feet started going way too fast, and by God's grace, I smashed into that fence. My dad was scared of what Momma would say. I also remember my dad treated my contusion with salt and butter. Another time, I got hit by a car while riding my bike; fortunately, the bike was the loser. Then, there was the time when we were playing baseball, and I was the catcher, and we didn't think to use face guards back then. This kid threw the bat, and it smacked me right in the mouth, broke several teeth, and left me with ten stitches on my lip. Another time, I was driving, and there came this shiny object bouncing my way. As it got closer, I could see it was a trailer truck's hubcap. At the very last moment, I swerved to the left after observing its trajectory. PANGGGG it went as it smashed into the guardrail. Whoosh, that was close. Let's not forget that dude in prison who came close to killing me as well. A few more inches, and he could have hit the artery near my neck.

During a summer day, I was getting dizzy while mowing the lawn. It took me much longer than usual. I ended up going to the emergency room, where doctors detected an enzyme the heart gives off when it's in distress. While I was hospitalized, I was given a cardiac cauterization. This is when they go through a main artery to look at the heart. After they finished this delicate procedure, they put a plug in that main artery. When released, I was instructed not to lift more than ten pounds because the pressure could force the plug to dislodge, and I could bleed out. Just three days out of the hospital, I was driving my car, and this kid without a license runs into me from behind. I managed to have the presence of mind to take my foot off the brake, brace for impact, and then stop the car gently. I'm glad to say it worked. This kid was going fast. He took his eyes off the road, and BAM! About $6000 in damages.

On another occasion, during a beautiful day at about 2:00 p.m., I was walking toward my car after ending my business day, which was on 52nd Street, West New York, New Jersey. I had just washed it, and it sparkled in the sun. There was a four-wheeler approaching, so I decided to let the driver go by, and then I'd cross the street. BAMMM! The driver took out the whole right side of my car. It was bad, some $7,000 in damages from the rear bumper to the front headlight. She claimed to have dozed off. Had I crossed the street or had I been there five seconds sooner, I would not be writing this book today. I'd say the worst accident occurred when I was leaving my job at 149th and Broadway in New York City, where I was the director of Federation & Guidance Services, Independent Living Housing Program. I got into my gear, and that's when the motorcycle accident that I referenced earlier occurred; it was equivalent to my knee exploding. Not only was the patella destroyed, but all surrounding tissue was severely traumatized. I was really afraid to get back on a motor bike for a while, but as they say, you have to get back on the horse. So after about a year, I purchased another Gixxer/GSXR street super sport racing bike. It felt great, but as usual, some reckless driver comes along and ruins things. One day, I was running a few errands and was lane-splitting a bit. This individual attempted to drive by me as the light turned green. He clipped my bike and ran over my right foot. I chased him down, and long story short, he was convicted of leaving the scene of an accident with bodily injury. He received a $500 fine, penalized with eight points on his license, lost his license for six months, and I'm sure his insurance company penalized him as well. At that point, I realized two more inches, and he would have taken out my leg.

Meanwhile, approximately eleven years had elapsed since my motorcycle accident, and my recovery was a difficult one. I went through five surgeries due to the Con Edison pothole accident. The first was a partial patellectomy, during which the knee surgeon fused the biggest bones together and extracted the small chips of broken bone. After about two years, I was still in too much pain, and he removed the whole thing during a full patellectomy. My knee looked bad and deformed, so I decided to get a prosthetic put in. Once again, they split me open, and the doctor sewed the prosthetic into place. About two days later, it was discovered that I had methicillin-resistant Staphylococcus aureus (MRSA), an infection. So, I was re-hospitalized, opened again, cleaned up, and then a pick line was inserted through a vein leading toward my heart. The reason for this was that the vancomycin was so strong it could burn my veins. I had to do two 800 mg dosages a day for eight weeks through an IV line hanging out of my arm. I thought everything was okay and began yet another four months of therapy, but something went wrong, and the prosthetic came loose and shifted to the right side of my knee; you could see the prong pushing up against the skin. I panicked and immediately ran to another surgeon. I told him I don't want nothing else introduced into my body; just take it out and let me live. He stated that the knee was extremely damaged and required a full knee replacement; thus, I should do it now while he was in there taking out the failed prosthetic. I agreed, and it was done.

In the end, they saved my leg, but I had constant pain. I couldn't run, jump, or aggressively use my leg. Every time I had a procedure, it was followed by four to six months of therapy. God always provided, and we never lacked anything. It was a period of several years of heavy pain killers and unbearable pain. My life was never the same, and I was classified as disabled. Through all the sickness and pain, I always repeated to myself, "His grace is sufficient, and I can do all things through Christ who strengthens me." I was in bed for months until one day, I decided if I was going to be lying there, I needed to do something with my time.

FINDING NEW PURPOSE

Life went on, and I continued trying to reach out to Jai and make contact. As the Bible commands, we relentlessly did our best to extend an olive branch, but she would have none of it. My wife, Cheyenne, and I would take several vacations a year all over the map, but Jai never accepted an invite. Each time we'd mange to invite her, she'd return a sarcastic, "I'm busy." My father died in February 2006, and we contacted her to give her the news. All my siblings flew out to Puerto Rico to lay him to rest. I offered to pay for her flight to Puerto Rico to pay her respects, but she refused. A short time later, my niece Katherine got married, and Jai refused to come to the wedding. Then, my other niece Alexandra got married, and again, Jai refused to attend as well. My other nephew Dave Jr. got married, and again, she refused to partake with the family. I was still determined to not give up on my child, so I continued to pray and asked others for prayer as well. Her Uncle Josh

(Bishop Rodriguez) had invited her and her young fiancé over to his home and had a talk with them. Josh later recalled how surprised his own daughters Gabriella and Daniella were to see her, as they never really knew of her existence. I was told Daniella constantly asked her, "Are you really my cousin?" and "Are you really Cheyenne's sister?" and "Tio Joel is really your father?" Perhaps, God was starting to soften her heart, or so it seemed. A few weeks later, Carmen and I invited Jai and her fiancé Orlando to dinner, and they accepted. During dinner, I wanted and attempted to get to know my future son-in-law, but the experience seemed awkward, and Jai was very evasive. Orlando was telling me about his desires to become a corrections officer and was perplexed that I was a chaplain at Hudson County Correctional with all the same rights and privileges as any other employee at the jail. My demeanor and life experience was not what he expected since I appeared to shatter an apparent false narrative he had heard about me. I couldn't put my finger on the weird feeling I had over her gleeful acceptance out to dinner until Jai began talking about her wedding expenses—of how she was in need of a television and a dining room set. The evening ended the way it began: strange and bizarre, but I thanked God for the opportunity to meet with her and her fiancé. Shortly thereafter, Jai accepted an invitation to our annual Rodriguez function, and I gifted her with a flat-screen TV. I felt as though we had finely turned the corner, and I was going to experience a fresh relationship with my daughter. I envisioned a new dimension of mutual communication, warmth, love, and care. My wife convinced her to go out to a Broadway musical with her and Cheyenne; God was turning things around. Then, she steadily dropped the hint about getting the wedding expenses and her wish that Cheyenne and Orlando's sister come out in the wedding. Everything was arranged and planned, and then, just like that, everything was canceled. Evidently, a family dispute among the bride and groom's respective families led to a wedding with no bridal party and a great number of family members not attending.

They had an exceptionally small wedding. She invited Cheyenne, Carmen, my mother, one of my siblings, and me. No aunts and no cousins. We accepted the invitation for several reasons. Jai is my daughter, and I love her. We wanted to do our best to restore our relationship despite the attempt by many to sabotage it. We also wanted to honor her and help her understand that transactional relationships are not healthy. I did not expect her to celebrate me at her wedding day, but I did expect her to acknowledge me as her biological father. Unfortunately, she demonstrated no honor, respect, or gratitude for being the vessel God used to bring her into this world. She had her second stepfather walk her down the aisle, engage in a prayer, and have the father-daughter dance. We sat there and prayed silently, knowing God was truly my redeemer, and I had nothing to worry about. We had always wished that she would have given me an opportunity to help give her the wedding of her dreams, but the opportunity was not given to me. We had sat there and observed the strange look on guests' faces who knew I was her biological father while her stepfather tried to play the role.

I was never an absentee father. I was a father who made poor choices and was sent to prison for seven vital years of my child's life. It was evident that the lack of child support during my time away was used against me, and a false narrative of abandonment was planted in my daughter's life as a result. During the festivities of the wedding, I simply sucked it up, took it all in, and did my best to portray I was happy.

A few weeks later, Cheyenne had a birthday, so I invited Jai to come over. She came to my home, but again, started acting peculiar. We attempted to speak with her, but it seemed she wasn't in the mood to communicate with us. She wouldn't answer questions or even engage in cordial conversation. I remember her getting up and leaving without even saying goodbye. I wondered and refused to believe that my daughter had simply resurfaced for more stuff. Not that I cared, it was just money, and I had plenty of it at the time.

Soon after these events, Jai began to display indifference and alienation again. I would send her friendly emails, and she would respond sarcastically. Then on Father's Day, I commented that it was sad that she had made a conscientious decision to ignore her biological father. She went off on a tangent about how I was not her father and simply a "sperm donor" and on and on. I realized then that it had all been another transactional tactic to acquire money and assets once again. As fathers we should provide no matter how indifferent kids may be, but everything has a limit. Needless to say, she went underground again and alienated everyone once more, including her innocent little sister. All we could do was continue to pray for deliverance and healing. The Bible clearly states in 2 Corinthians 10:3–5, "For though we walk in the flesh, we do not war according to the flesh. For the weapons of our warfare *are* not carnal but mighty in God for pulling down strongholds, casting down arguments and every high thing that exalts itself against the knowledge of God, bringing every thought into captivity to the obedience of Christ." Looking back, I had a really bad vibe, and my antenna for transactional people had been activated, but I love my daughter and gave her the benefit of the doubt.

By now, many were aware that Jai's strange and ambiguous behavior was as complicated as her mother's, but like any caring biological parent, I refused to give up on my child and stood on God's Word. Despite the indifference, lack of respect, outright rejection, and alienation toward me, her stepmom, sister, paternal cousins, aunts and uncles, and two God-fearing grandparents, we still prayed for a breakthrough. Despite my personal feelings and the pain that this has caused, I've never regretted conceiving a child with Esperanza, for this was all God's plan to create Jaivyn, Ava, and Ezra—my grandchildren. Despite the treatment that I had received from Jai and her mother, God's hand was in all of this. God makes no mistakes. In fact, even when we make mistakes, he is able to turn things around. Hebrews 4:12 says, "For the word of God is living and active, sharper than any two-edged sword, piercing to the division of soul and of spirit, of joints and of marrow, and discerning the thoughts and intentions of the heart."

These events and occurrences may sound shocking, and some may say that I was to blame for it all. Perhaps it may all sound too outrageous to be true. Every family has issues and dysfunctions, including mine. I once heard someone say that nothing happens in a vacuum. Every attitude and behavior is rooted in things that we previously learned. My attempt is not to throw "shade" on anybody; I am simply trying to convey a painful story and how God, in his mercy, has seen me through my pain and given me an opportunity to forgive and surrender many things to Him. For many years, I thought I was the sole problem and that my issues were primarily to blame for my challenging relationship with my daughter Jai. The fact is that through the years, I have discovered that Jai's maternal family have had all types of family disputes resulting in the use of alienation as a defense mechanism. Some time ago, Jai's younger brother publicly shared on social media some of the pain, drama, and unnecessary conflicts caused by his own biological parents. The young man sounded sincere; on the other hand, however, Esperanza made a decision to engage in alienation and hurt many people along the way, including my children. She has never told me what led to her apparent decision to emotionally and physically separate me from my child despite my constant financial support. Family is to be loved and cherished. The Bible says in Matthew 5, "But I say unto you, love your enemies, bless them that curse you, do good to them that hate you, and pray for them which despitefully use you, and persecute you." In other words, build bridges; don't burn them. No one, including myself, has ever been told the reason why Esperanza psychologically abused and mistreated my child. No one may ever know. Why would anyone choose to inflict pain and anguish on a loving father and a wonderful family? No child deserves to be brainwashed, confused, and manipulated with lies and falsehoods for selfish and self-serving purposes. Additionally, if a parent was unfit, what would be the cause for wiping away the connection that the child has to its entire paternal family. Any desire to possess a child and deprive them blessings from a loving nurturing family is unhealthy.

Jai's emotional conditioning began young. When she challenged her mother and questioned any contradictions, she was threatened and chastised. She was never able to trust in herself as a child and unable to acquire building blocks for a healthy perspective. A child's developing mind is fragile, and it should be criminal to exploit them, but as I'm a witness, it happens all too often. Children are empty, gullible vessels. They are innocent and pure. The correct decision should have been shielding the child instead of utilizing her as a tool. My heart was seriously conflicted because I knew these children had suffered. I theorize this is the maddening confusion that young Ramón (Jai's maternal brother) felt and was haunted by until he truly realized the hurt that his parents caused others. He wrote a letter on social media, apologizing for his mother and stepfather's misdeeds. He ended his letter by asking for forgiveness on their behalf and admitting they would never be capable of asking for forgiveness themselves. As for me, I sought forgiveness and reconciliation for years. I have prayed without ceasing and cried until I couldn't anymore. I have begged until I could no longer beg. Finally, I took the pain, anguish, and sorrow and gave it all to God; He officially had all my burdens cast upon Him.

I have been blessed beyond measure and, as I mentioned previously, had made some arrangements for my grandchildren, Jai, Ava, and Ezra. My hope is that one day, they learn about their true and valid biological paternal family and Satan's tactics to divide, alienate, and separate family. Hopefully, they will also learn about how God commands us all to honor our biological parents despite their flaws. Hopefully, one day, they will learn about their potential spiritual, familial, and economic blessings. My hope and prayer is that one day, they learn the truth.

No one should ever have to experience the pain of alienation and denial, but I did. Just as I was denied visitation when Jai was a child, now the cycle has repeated itself once more. Despite the pain that this has caused me, I am at peace, and I have decided to forgive and lean on God as my healer.

CONCLUSION

God's faithfulness is amazing. Despite all of our struggles, God will never let us down. Despite the attacks that Satan brings our way, even through people who we love, God will always carry us through our trials, protect, defend, and heal us.

My beautiful daughter, Cheyenne, graduated high school and went off to UConn. Jai, as usual, didn't have any contact. Life went on, and we didn't hear from her. Countless attempts by my younger brother and other family members proved beyond futile, and slowly, she went from distant memory to Jai who? Then, in 2020, both my mother-in-law and my mother passed to be with the Lord within weeks of each other. As you may have guessed, Jai refused to call her sister or any member of the family to offer condolences. I believe that these moments of love and compassion that enveloped my family also bought clarity. The matriarch was gone, and what had survived was an ever-growing blessed family of loving and faithful children who lacked nothing. We laid our mothers to rest and realized it had come time to be at peace with Jai's decisions too. As time went on, Cheyenne had transferred from UConn to Rutgers. We sold our old home and built a new one. Cheyenne graduated summa cum laude with her bachelor's degree, and we celebrated her mightily. Cheyenne had invited her friends and family to attend the ceremonies, and we partied. I refused to sit and fantasize about the impossible and continue to concentrate on my relationship with God and reality. We had collectively prayed for over thirty years against division, separation, hate, bitterness, and resentment and understood God had provided the answer years ago. Sadly, my daughter Jai has remained distant from our family, creating a void that we have had to entrust fully to God. Her absence, though deeply felt, has become a part of our lives that we've learned to accept with grace and peace. We take comfort in knowing she and her children are alive, well, and living their own journey. In the meantime, God has been overwhelmingly good to us, blessing our family in incredible ways. He has filled our lives with joy, laughter, and new beginnings, surrounding us with little ones raised by parents who welcome love and faith into their homes. Though I've never considered myself someone who naturally gravitates toward babies, the depth of love God has placed in my heart for others—children and adults alike—has been transformative. When I love, I love fully and without reservation. While I have not been given the opportunity to share that love personally with Jai and her children, my prayers for them remain constant, and my trust in God's timing unwavering. I refuse to allow pain to dictate my actions or to respond with anything but love. Our family has shown tremendous love and care, offering connection through fourteen aunts and uncles, thirteen cousins, nine great cousins, and countless others. Although the response was not what we had hoped for, we continue to trust God's greater plan, knowing He works all things together for good.

The Bible tells us of a man who sold his blessings for some food. Genesis 25 says, "Jacob said, 'Sell me your birthright now.' Esau said, 'I am about to die; of what use is a birthright to me?' Jacob said, 'Swear to me now.' So, he swore to him and sold his birthright to Jacob. Then Jacob gave Esau bread and lentil stew, and he ate and drank and rose and went his way." Sheer bananas! This would be today's equivalent of giving away your family inheritance for social media "likes." I can't help but chuckle at the sheer stupidity of it all, but hey, some people do the unimaginable. What the devil meant for harm, God uses for good. So, as it turned out, Jai was fuel for the next generation of Martinez kids. They suddenly realized if one of their own could rise in the ranks of academics and professionalism, they understood it was possible for them too. I've seen a change in the Martinez family because of Jai's academic success, so I am content with what the Lord has done and how He's done it. I assume the moral of the story could be: don't sweat the details and rely on God for answers. He said it in Psalm 94:14: "For the LORD will not forsake his people; he will not abandon his heritage." Philippians 4:6–7 says, "Do not be anxious about anything, but in everything by prayer and supplication with thanksgiving let your requests be made known to God. And the peace of God, which surpasses all understanding, will guard your hearts and your minds in Christ Jesus." And James 1:17 says, "Every good gift and every perfect gift is from above, coming down from the Father of lights with whom there is no variation or shadow due to change." So, rejoice and be glad; rejoice for all God has given you, for the good and the bad; it all works together, and in the end, it was all His plan, after all.

Love conquers hate, and evil can never defeat goodness, though it may try. Have you ever thought about the scary reality that full grown adults can be fooled, controlled, manipulated, and misled like sheep? In studying human behavior, what was truly revealing and frightening to me was the mind-control tactics that took place during 2016. It was a strange time in America. The manner in which someone could proclaim himself as "the chosen one" and con millions still fascinates me. In the end, he left a legendary mess and conned thousands, over 1,100 of whom went to jail, thus far obeying his foolish, psychotic, and misguided orders.

Matthew 24:24 says, "For false Christs and false prophets will arise and will show great signs and wonders, so as to mislead, if possible, even the elect." The sad reality was that this wasn't the first time a person or group was brainwashed or conditioned to believe falsehoods and fantasies. During November

18, 1978, Jim Jones, who was best known for being an American cult leader who promised his followers a utopia in the jungles of South America after proclaiming himself messiah of the Peoples Temple, a San Francisco-based evangelist group, ultimately led his followers into a mass suicide, which left more than 900 dead and came to be known as the Jonestown Massacre. Further, on March 19–20, 1997, Marshall Applewhite taped himself in *Do's Final Exit*, speaking of mass suicide and "the only way to evacuate this Earth." After asserting that Comet Hale–Bopp was the sign that the group had been looking for, as well as speculation that an unidentified flying object (UFO) may have been trailing the comet, Applewhite and his thirty-eight followers prepared for ritual suicide so their souls could reach the Next Level before the closure of "Heaven's Gate." Members believed that after their deaths, a UFO would take their souls to another "level of existence above human," which Applewhite described as being both physical and spiritual. Their preparations included each member videotaping a farewell message.

To kill themselves, members took phenobarbital mixed with apple sauce or pudding and washed it down with vodka. After ingesting the applesauce/pudding mix, they secured plastic bags around their heads to induce asphyxiation. All thirty-nine were dressed in identical black shirts and sweat pants, brand new black-and-white Nike Decades athletic shoes, and armband patches reading «Heaven›s Gate Away Team." Sadly, the list of those duped goes on and on.

Just imagine cops, military, and other adults who were gullible enough to obey such lies and silliness, grown folks, husbands, wives, gullible and stupid enough to obey a man's madness and concocted fantasies. So, in the end, I've come to understand that there are grown folks falling for cons and smoke and mirrors and adults filled with plain abject stupidity, falling prey to ignorant propaganda and fairytale falsehoods.

I can now understand how my daughter Jai may have been manipulated and deceived. She was indoctrinated when she was very young, day by day, week by week, month by month, and year after year until the brainwashing was complete. It's a sad reality; grown people made fools and gullible, willing cult members in just a few years, acting like mind-controlled individuals. Just like the antichrist is to be worshiped, they put his mark on their lawns, trucks, and foreheads. Many even went out recruiting for their calling in life. Some even called their leader their messiah and placed him ahead of God Almighty. Our nation was polarized and beyond confused. However, when you're a child of God, you're supposed to guard your heart and mind from all methods of evil. The experience of watching someone con adult people helped me to understand how my kid was so mentally impacted, but it doesn't excuse her willingness to believe the lies regardless of the contradictory evidence before her when she grew older. I understand as a child, it was easier to accept the lies and ignore the truth. It's never okay to listen to madness and pretend to hear and accept absurdities and agree. It's not okay to swallow questionable information without asking questions. Only cults are built in this manner; control can only function with dangerously brainwashed cult members. One's life is usually built on relationships and love, yet only a confused person would "throw the baby out with the bath water," "burn bridges," or even worse, "sell their inheritance."

I conclude by conveying my heartfelt prayers to all of you, your family, and your grandchildren. I can honestly say I am at peace and blessed despite never having met my grandchildren. In fact, my entire family is blessed and highly favored by God Almighty. It's hard to miss what you never had. Therefore, my joy comes from the Lord, and I rejoice knowing that I am free from having anyone use children as weapons against me or anyone in my family. My heartfelt prayer is that you all love and hold your children tightly, especially if you are a young parent and grew up in a divorced household. Don't bite the hand that feeds you, respect and honor your biological parents (both of them), and never choose sides. Don't act foolishly and curse your inheritance and negatively impact your children in a similar manner. Allow your children to receive the blessings you rejected and learn to love everyone, regardless of the nonsense a family member may tell you. Satan really tried to stifle our family. We wept over the lack of connection and mourned the loss, but when you release it to God, He takes what the enemy meant for evil and turns it around for good. Lastly, to my grandkids, we'll catch up in heaven, and remember, God will honor you if you honor your parents (even the ones you are not able to comprehend), but beware because no one knows what awaits you if you choose the path of the prodigal son and don't return home! Parents, remember to raise your children to love and respect, and teach them to honor family.

Luke 15:11–24 says,

> And he said, "There was a man who had two sons. And the younger of them said to his father, 'Father, give me the share of property that is coming to me.' And he divided his property between them. Not many days later, the younger son gathered all he had and took a journey into a far country, and there he squandered his property in reckless living. And when he had spent everything, a severe famine arose in that country, and he began to be in need. So he went and hired himself out to one of the citizens of that country, who sent him into his fields to feed pigs... But when he came to himself, he said, 'How many of my father's hired servants have more than enough bread, but I perish here with hunger! I will arise and go to my father, and I will say to him, "Father, I have sinned against heaven and before you. I am no longer worthy to be called your son. Treat me as one of your hired servants."' And he arose and

came to his father. But while he was still a long way off, his father saw him and felt compassion, and ran and embraced him and kissed him. 'Your brother has come,' he replied, 'and your father has killed the fattened calf because he has him back safe and sound.' The older brother became angry and refused to go in. So his father went out and pleaded with him, but he answered his father, 'Look! All these years I've been slaving for you and never disobeyed your orders. Yet you never gave me even a young goat so I could celebrate with my friends. But when this son of yours who has squandered your property with prostitutes comes home, you kill the fattened calf for him! My son,' the father said, 'you are always with me, and everything I have is yours. But we had to celebrate and be glad, because this brother of yours was dead and is alive again; he was lost and is found.'"

My hope is that every wayward child comes back home, but the reality is that some kids never find their way back home. That is my story. Jai never came back home, and even worse, she refused to receive her inheritance.

God Almighty, who first loved us, commands us to love everyone. However, at times, love may be responded to with hate, bitterness, resentment, vengeance, and evil. When healing does not take place in the life of any person, then children can be used as pawns and weapons. God is more than able to heal wounded hearts, and if you suspect that a person has experienced trauma, then therapy can serve as a vehicle to assist that person with their healing. If you know someone going before a judge in family court, you may want to suggest that they ask the court to mandate therapy. The court system can also serve by highlighting what healthy adult responsibilities entail. Since most children respond well to adults with authority, the court mediation serves as a witness since everything is documented. The effort to seek outside help when dealing with major conflict may be invaluable. In my story, my prodigal daughter never returned, scorned her family, cursed the blessing and inheritance, and never received it. She then repeated the cycle, deprived her kids of their inheritance, and essentially saddled them with a generational curse unleashed on her years earlier. Always remember God knows what is best for you, and He'll remove what is not, and above all things, don't be stupid! Your children are not ammunition or weapons in your personal war and vendetta. Lastly, trust in the Lord always and be wise.

Sincerely,

I end with this; I have tried to convey my life experiences to the best of my ability and with an honest and contrite heart. Some experiences I look back upon and realize God's mercy and grace were with me; like a concerned Father, He watched from afar. I recognize now as the Bible states in Genesis 50:20, "As for you, you meant evil against me, but God meant it for good in order to bring about this present result, to preserve many people alive." I look back at my turmoil with joy, understanding today that with each and every battle, I was molded and shaped in the likeness and image of God. Romans 5:3 says, "Not only so, but we also glory in our sufferings, because we know that suffering produces perseverance; perseverance, character; and character, hope." I no longer find meaning in weeping for days that have gone by, and instead, I embrace the peace that surpasses all understanding. I now comprehend why the Lord allowed me to experience those painful and long years of depravation, isolation, and humiliation to mold me. He had prepared me for future battles and warfare with the weapons I needed. He strengthened my soul and prepared my mind and spirit for what was to come. The ordeal of losing my child was painful, and the trauma of alienation was cruel. The disrespect was appalling, but God's hand was in all of it, and He never left me nor abandoned me during the process. He kept His promises, and I'm here to tell you that just as He did it for Job, He did it for me. As the Holy Scripture says in Psalm 30:5, "Weeping may tarry for the night, but joy comes with the morning." My whole life story has led me to this moment, which I embrace and proclaim could only be possible by God's almighty grace, and I am at peace. I feel sanctified and glorify God every day. In further retrospect, much of my life was filled with opportunities for Satan to end my existence and confine me to eternity in hell, yet God's merciful hand spared me and created a living testimony. In turn, although I am still a work in progress, I have been given the responsibility to share the Good News of the gospel and tell of the greatness of God. My story began with the description of my own life as a defiant child who saw no value to education or the path of righteousness, but God turned everything around. After God allowed me to go through the winepress and baptism with fire, I have emerged as a product of the Most High God. You may see some of yourself in some of my trials and tribulations and wonder how you'd survive if faced with similar dilemmas. The fact is that God has a unique set of circumstances that He allows each of us to go through. Each of us has a unique capacity to endure the process that God puts before us, and each of us is uniquely built to withstand it; thus, every process is exclusive to the individual. The irony is that when I was lost in darkness, I never considered doing physical harm to people, but I did. I never thought of associating with drug lords and street hoods, but I did. And now God has used those haunting memories to remind me of His mighty, merciful hand. The firsthand experiences of an individual can be more useful and significant than the volumes of materials they study and learn about. Today, my words flow from a place of contrition and repentance after the depths of heartache and depression. I reached up, and Jesus saved me and pulled me out of my mess. During a dark period in my life, I found myself habitually using cocaine and alcohol, but God reached down and restored me to a place of freedom, honor, and peace. Kicking drugs wasn't easy, but with God, all things are possible. I could not have done it alone, and honestly, the twelve steps can only get you so far, and believe me, you're going to need a lot more than twelve steps. The philosophy of one day at a time is only good for the first week, then its week after week, month after month, and some of you know the rest; thus, one slip, one drink, one sniff or puff, and all that success goes down the tubes. Just like the story of Lot's wife, who followed behind him (foolishly, longingly), looked (back toward Sodom in an act of disobedience), and she became a pillar of salt. Let us not look back; there may have been fun times, but those sinful experiences were not pleasing to God. I don't miss any of the madness, and my questionable health issues are reminders of the precarious and destructive experiences I had. My career in mental health has been instrumental in keeping me sane, stable, and open to improving on all that God has entrusted to me. It is by God's grace, wisdom, and glory that I stand before you. Today, I am so thankful that God has spared my life. Had it not been for God today, I might have been a single, unemployed, and homeless ex-con with a severe drug addiction and depression. "Thank you, Father God, because you first loved me." I would not be alive had it not been for God, who has filled my life with love, peace, and purpose despite my challenging journey. I continue to strive for the heart of David and preach the gospel always, and only when necessary, as a famous preacher said, "with words." Life is a beautiful thing; don't waste it on regrets. You are valuable and priceless, and that is why you have been made in the image and likeness of God. Trust in God always, for if He is for you, nothing can stand against you. If you've never known Jesus as your Lord, thy God, it's not too late. Accept Him into your heart and repent for your sins and transgressions. Lay all your cares at the altar and receive rest and the peace that surpasses all understanding. Promise to walk according to the gospel of Jesus Christ. Acknowledge that Jesus died on the cross and was raised from the dead. Surrender your life to the Lord, and He will lead you down the path of righteousness.

ABOUT THE AUTHOR

Joel Rodríguez is currently the director of Cityline Church Prison Outreach Program in Jersey City, New Jersey. Joel is a seasoned behavioral/social science administrator with over thirty years of expertise in crisis management and treatment modalities. He has vast professional experience in various fields of mental health, including as a preventive case worker/case planner for United Families of East Harlem (Div. of Edwin Gould), New York, New York; Kinship Foster Home case worker for New York Catholic Guardian Society; Senior Eviction Prevention case manager at the Community Service Society of New York; resident manager at Federation Employment & Guidance Services; program director of the New Jersey Community Development Corporation; preventive supervisor at the Salvation Army/Morris Heights Center for Families; and Mobile Response clinician for Catholic Charities of the Archdiocese of Newark.

Additionally, he is professionally adaptable and has filled many positions, from case manager, resident manager, supervisor, and director for a large mental health organization. He has also supervised multiple staff throughout the foster care system.

Joel is a man of faith and a minister, leader, husband, father, brother, grandfather, and friend. He is a man of integrity and character, which is exemplified through his walk with Jesus Christ. Joel's testimony bears witness that all things are possible to those who believe. He has lived a life filled with incidents that have included long years of incarceration, as well as battles with mental health and narcotics. God has been faithful during this entire process, and through favor, grace, and determination, Joel has completed his master's degree in human services, bachelor's degree from Marist College, paralegal certification, criminal justice certification, and is a certified crisis intervention specialist, among other achievements.

www.ingramcontent.com/pod-product-compliance
Lightning Source LLC
Chambersburg PA
CBHW061247140726
47998CB00006B/2132